OPPOSING
VIEWPOINTS®
SERIES

Organ Donation

Other Books of Related Interest

Opposing Viewpoints Series

Genetic Engineering
Health Care
Medical Technology

At Issue Series

Embryonic and Adult Stem Cells
Extending the Human Life Span
Organ Transplants

Current Controversies Series

Human Trafficking
Medicare
Vaccines

"Congress shall make no law … abridging the freedom of speech, or of the press."

First Amendment to the US Constitution

The basic foundation of our democracy is the First Amendment guarantee of freedom of expression. The Opposing Viewpoints Series is dedicated to the concept of this basic freedom and the idea that it is more important to practice it than to enshrine it.

OPPOSING VIEWPOINTS® SERIES

Organ Donation

Laura Egendorf, Book Editor

GREENHAVEN PRESS
A part of Gale, Cengage Learning

GALE
CENGAGE Learning

Detroit • New York • San Francisco • New Haven, Conn • Waterville, Maine • London

Elizabeth Des Chenes, *Director, Publishing Solutions*

© 2013 Greenhaven Press, a part of Gale, Cengage Learning

Gale and Greenhaven Press are registered trademarks used herein under license.

For more information, contact:
Greenhaven Press
27500 Drake Rd.
Farmington Hills, MI 48331-3535
Or you can visit our Internet site at gale.cengage.com.

For product information and technology assistance, contact us at:

Gale Customer Support, 1-800-877-4253.
For permission to use material from this text or product, submit all requests online at www.cengage.com/permissions.

Further permissions questions can be emailed to permissionrequest@cengage.com.

Articles in Greenhaven Press anthologies are often edited for length to meet page requirements. In addition, original titles of these works are changed to clearly present the main thesis and to explicitly indicate the author's opinion. Every effort is made to ensure that Greenhaven Press accurately reflects the original intent of the authors. Every effort has been made to trace the owners of copyrighted material.

Cover Image © Jeff Banke/Shutterstock.com.

LIBRARY OF CONGRESS CATALOGING-IN-PUBLICATION DATA

Organ donation / Laura Egendorf, book editor.
     pages cm. -- (Opposing viewpoints)
   Includes bibliographical references and index.
   ISBN 978-0-7377-6332-4 (hardcover) -- ISBN 978-0-7377-6333-1 (pbk.)
  1. Donation of organs, tissues, etc.--Popular works. I. Egendorf, Laura K., 1973-
   RD129.5.O738 2013
   362.17'83--dc23

2013002332

Printed in the United States of America
  1 2 3 4 5   17 16 15 14 13

Contents

Chapter 1: Is the Organ Allocation System Fair?

Chapter 2: How Can Organ Donation Be Increased?

Why Consider Opposing Viewpoints?

> "The only way in which a human being can make some approach to knowing the whole of a subject is by hearing what can be said about it by persons of every variety of opinion and studying all modes in which it can be looked at by every character of mind. No wise man ever acquired his wisdom in any mode but this."
>
> *John Stuart Mill*

In our media-intensive culture it is not difficult to find differing opinions. Thousands of newspapers and magazines and dozens of radio and television talk shows resound with differing points of view. The difficulty lies in deciding which opinion to agree with and which "experts" seem the most credible. The more inundated we become with differing opinions and claims, the more essential it is to hone critical reading and thinking skills to evaluate these ideas. Opposing Viewpoints books address this problem directly by presenting stimulating debates that can be used to enhance and teach these skills. The varied opinions contained in each book examine many different aspects of a single issue. While examining these conveniently edited opposing views, readers can develop critical thinking skills such as the ability to compare and contrast authors' credibility, facts, argumentation styles, use of persuasive techniques, and other stylistic tools. In short, the Opposing Viewpoints Series is an ideal way to attain the higher-level thinking and reading skills so essential in a culture of diverse and contradictory opinions.

In addition to providing a tool for critical thinking, Opposing Viewpoints books challenge readers to question their own strongly held opinions and assumptions. Most people form their opinions on the basis of upbringing, peer pressure, and personal, cultural, or professional bias. By reading carefully balanced opposing views, readers must directly confront new ideas as well as the opinions of those with whom they disagree. This is not to argue simplistically that everyone who reads opposing views will—or should—change his or her opinion. Instead, the series enhances readers' understanding of their own views by encouraging confrontation with opposing ideas. Careful examination of others' views can lead to the readers' understanding of the logical inconsistencies in their own opinions, perspective on why they hold an opinion, and the consideration of the possibility that their opinion requires further evaluation.

Evaluating Other Opinions

To ensure that this type of examination occurs, Opposing Viewpoints books present all types of opinions. Prominent spokespeople on different sides of each issue as well as well-known professionals from many disciplines challenge the reader. An additional goal of the series is to provide a forum for other, less known, or even unpopular viewpoints. The opinion of an ordinary person who has had to make the decision to cut off life support from a terminally ill relative, for example, may be just as valuable and provide just as much insight as a medical ethicist's professional opinion. The editors have two additional purposes in including these less known views. One, the editors encourage readers to respect others' opinions—even when not enhanced by professional credibility. It is only by reading or listening to and objectively evaluating others' ideas that one can determine whether they are worthy of consideration. Two, the inclusion of such viewpoints encourages the important critical thinking skill of objectively evaluating an author's credentials and bias. This evaluation will illuminate an author's reasons for taking a particular stance on an issue and will aid in readers' evaluation of the author's ideas.

It is our hope that these books will give readers a deeper understanding of the issues debated and an appreciation of the complexity of even seemingly simple issues when good and honest people disagree. This awareness is particularly important in a democratic society such as ours in which people enter into public debate to determine the common good. Those with whom one disagrees should not be regarded as enemies but rather as people whose views deserve careful examination and may shed light on one's own.

Thomas Jefferson once said that "difference of opinion leads to inquiry, and inquiry to truth." Jefferson, a broadly educated man, argued that "if a nation expects to be ignorant and free . . . it expects what never was and never will be." As individuals and as a nation, it is imperative that we consider the opinions of others and examine them with skill and discernment. The Opposing Viewpoints Series is intended to help readers achieve this goal.

David L. Bender and Bruno Leone,
Founders

Introduction

"Facebook's goal to help solve the problem of organ donation is laudable, but to be effective users will have to embrace the idea of sharing information that some may see as incredibly personal."

Ian Paul, PCWorld, *May 1, 2012.*

One of the challenges facing organ donation is finding ways to educate people on the need for organ donors and how they can become potential donors. The most effective solutions may involve the Internet, as hundreds of millions of people can be reached in an instant. On May 1, 2012, the social network behemoth Facebook suggested a new way to harness the power of social media when it introduced a feature that lets people sign up as organ donors. However, questions remain as to whether social media is an effective long-term answer for the shortage in donor organs and whether people who participate in these programs could risk a loss of privacy.

At Facebook's organ donation page, members can register as organ donors and share their organ donor status with other Facebook members. The page also details why the company decided to add this option, asserting:

> More than 114,000 people in the United States, and millions more around the globe, are waiting for the heart, kidney or liver transplant that will save their lives. Many of those people—an average of 18 people per day—will die waiting, because there simply aren't enough organ donors to meet the need. Medical experts believe that broader awareness about organ donation could go a long way toward solving this crisis.

Given that Facebook has one billion members worldwide, this initiative could potentially impact many lives. In fact, the immediate results were impressive. In their article in the *Hastings Center Report*, "Can Social Media Increase Transplant Donation and Save Lives?," Blair L. Sadler and Alfred M. Sadler Jr. write:

> What has happened after the May 1 announcement? According to David Fleming, CEO of Donate Life America, the initial response "dwarfs any past organ donation initiative." By the end of the day of the announcement, 6,000 people had enrolled through 22 state registries. Charlene Zettel, the CEO of Donate California, reported that California had experienced a remarkable uptick. Typically, about 70 people register as organ donors online each day; in the 24 hours following the Facebook announcement, about 3,900 Californians signed up.

Beyond Facebook's efforts, there have also been smaller regional programs that are trying to use social media and the Internet to increase the numbers of people registering as organ donors. For example, the Center for Donation and Transplant (CDT), a federal organization that coordinates the recovery of donated organs and tissues in northeastern New York and western Vermont, worked with a social media company to increase awareness of Vermont's online registry; its six-month effort resulted in a 525 percent increase in donor registrants.

However, these social media efforts may not be sustainable. The Sadler brothers observed that the Facebook impact lasted only two weeks, before organ registrant numbers returned to their pre-May 2012 numbers. Meanwhile, Vermont's numbers rose, but the state still has the lowest percentage of potential organ donors, at only 3 percent. Facebook has countered these assertions, pointing out that 275,000 people registered worldwide between May and September 2012. Still, for social networking to be a long-term answer to the organ shortage, further steps may need to be made. For example, Facebook could develop ways for people to share how organ donation has impacted their lives or the lives of relatives and friends. The Sadlers offer several further suggestions, including having state donor organizations provide Facebook with real-time updates on the number of donors; they also suggest that state registries need to be more user-friendly. Facebook is also working on a version of its organ donation page for mobile phones, which would make signing up even easier.

However, there could be drawbacks to involving social networks in the organ donation process. The growth of the Internet has been paralleled by an increase in the loss of privacy, with many people being too quick to reveal personal information that could fall into the wrong hands. In an article for the Internal Medicine News Digital Network, Miriam E. Tucker addresses this concern. She cites a study of Facebook pages that were seeking a living kidney donor for a specific person, either for themselves, a family member, or friend. The study found that the people creating these pages often included detailed medical histories and photographs, perhaps not understanding the potential risk of making such personal information available to the general public—particularly because the content of those pages is not covered by US medical privacy laws.

At the same time, these concerns about privacy could be overstated. The Internet may have made lives less private, but it could also be argued that people who belong to social networking sites have come to accept the tradeoff of less privacy for more information. Matthew Weinstock, senior editor of *Hospitals and Health Networks* magazine, observes, "As [Facebook founder Mark] Zuckerberg so poetically stated a couple of years ago, privacy is 'no longer a social norm.' The challenge, it seems, for the health care industry, is how to navigate this landscape that seems to change in the blink of eye."

The approach that Facebook is taking to increase the number of organ donors may be controversial, but it has also helped increase awareness about the need for organs. *Opposing Viewpoints: Organ Donation* examines the issues surrounding organ donation in the following chapters: Is the Organ Allocation System

Fair?, How Can Organ Donation Be Increased?, What Ethical Issues Surround Organ Donation?, and What Is the Future of Organ Donation? Authors explore, among other issues, the challenges of finding organs for those who need them while also considering the rights of potential donors and recipients.

CHAPTER 1

Is the Organ Allocation System Fair?

Chapter Preface

A major concern that many people have about the US organ transplantation system is whether organs reach the people most in need. The March 2012 heart transplant surgery of former US vice president Dick Cheney raised questions concerning both Cheney's fame and his age—and the impact those two factors may have had on his surgery.

Cheney was seventy-one and had had five heart attacks—and surgery to implant a partial artificial heart—before the transplant. Heart transplants for patients over the age of sixty-five are rare but not uncommon—332 out of 2,332 people in that age group received transplants in 2011, according to the United Network for Organ Sharing. One reason that relatively few older patients receive heart transplants is because recipients can have no other health problems, such as liver or lung damage—a state of good health that becomes less likely as patients age.

In the opinion of bioethicist Art Caplan, the vice president's operation was troubling not just because of his age—more than 3,100 people are on the waiting list for a heart, with most up to twenty years Cheney's junior—but also because his wealth and top-of-the-line health insurance gave him advantages most people don't have. According to Caplan, in a post on the NBC News blog *Vitals*, "It is possible that Cheney was the only person waiting for a heart who was a good match in terms of the donor's size, blood type and other biological and geographical factors. If not, then some tough ethical questions need to be asked. When all are asked to be organ donors, both rich and poor, shouldn't each one of us have a fair shot at getting a heart?"

However, not everyone agrees that Cheney had advantages unavailable to most potential organ recipients. Cheney was on the waiting list for twenty months, which is considerably longer than the average wait of six months to one year. On the blog *Postmodern Conservative*, Peter Lawler argues: "Did he cut in line? Is he too old? Nobody, in my opinion, should be asking such questions. He's too visible a guy to have been able to cut in line. Twenty months is a long wait—one that was pretty close to too long for Cheney. There appears to be nothing much physically wrong with Cheney beyond a long-standing bum ticker."

The debate over Dick Cheney's heart transplant is a microcosm of the issues surrounding the fairness of the US organ transplant system. In the following chapter, authors debate whether organ allocation is fair and discuss ways in which the system can be improved.

> *"[US government agencies] recognize the gaps in oversight that existed when serious problems were exposed at transplant centers."*

Government Oversight into Organ Transplants Needs Improvement

United States Government Accountability Office

In the following viewpoint, the United States Government Accountability Office (GAO) asserts that several government agencies must work together to improve government oversight into organ transplants and reduce the wait time for transplants. The GAO believes that the Centers for Medicare and Medicaid Services (CMS), the Organ Procurement and Transplantation Network (OPTN), and the Health Resources and Services Administration (HRSA) need to address problems such as understaffing, inadequate internal communication, and failure to protect living donors. According to the GAO, sharing information among the three agencies will help them reach this goal. The GAO is an independent, nonpartisan agency that works for Congress; its primary mission is to investigate how the federal government spends taxpayer dollars.

United States Government Accountability Office, "Organ Transplant Programs: Federal Agencies Have Acted to Improve Oversight, but Implementation Issues Remain," April 2008, pp. 13, 24–20.

As you read, consider the following questions:

1. According to the GAO, why did OPTN increase its staff size in 2007?
2. Why is it important for CMS and OPTN to exchange information on their oversight activities, per the GAO?
3. What is the difficult challenge facing CMS and HRSA, in GAO's opinion?

CMS's [Centers for Medicare and Medicaid Services] and, to a lesser extent, the OPTN's [Organ Procurement and Transplantation Network] oversight of transplant programs was not comprehensive at the time high-profile problems came to light in 2005 and 2006. CMS did not actively monitor extra-renal [non-kidney] transplant programs' compliance with criteria for Medicare approval. CMS monitored renal transplant programs through contracts with state agencies, but the surveys reviewed compliance with requirements that had not been substantially updated in decades and were limited in scope; also, not all programs were actively monitored. At the same time, the OPTN actively monitored transplant programs and took action to resolve identified problems, but its oversight activities fell short in some respects—the OPTN's monitoring did not include methods capable of promptly detecting problems at transplant programs that prolonged the time that patients waited for transplants, and the OPTN did not always meet its goals for conducting on-site reviews. . . .

Developing a Set of Indicators

To address shortcomings in the OPTN's ability to detect problems affecting patients waiting for transplants, such as understaffing, the OPTN and HRSA [Health Resources and Services Administration], along with another HRSA contractor, are working to develop and implement a set of activity-level indicators. The set of indicators would be used to monitor programs for problems, such as understaffing, indicated by lower-than-expected activity levels in a manner similar to how the OPTN currently monitors programs for performance problems indicated by lower-than-expected survival rates. The set of indicators includes two existing indicators already developed by the OPTN, one of which, although available, was not previously reviewed by the MPSC [Membership Professional Standards Committee], and a new organ acceptance rate indicator. The new indicator, which is intended to identify programs exhibiting lower-than-expected rates of organ acceptance, is a key component of the set of activity-level indicators and has been under development since January 2006. According to the OPTN, the organ acceptance rate indicator had been developed but not yet implemented for kidney and liver transplant programs as of February 2008.

With HRSA's encouragement, the OPTN has also taken steps to increase its capacity to conduct on-site monitoring activities and to improve internal communication. The OPTN substantially increased its staff in 2007 in order to get back on schedule in conducting on-site reviews once every 3 years. According to OPTN officials, the increase in staff will also help the OPTN address its backlog of peer review site visits and achieve its goal of conducting all peer review site visits within 3 months of the visit being recommended by the MPSC. To improve internal communication, the OPTN reported that since 2006, its leadership has emphasized the importance of shared communication, particularly across departments. As a result, according to the OPTN, staff responsible for managing the waiting list, including handling patient transfers, now meet frequently with staff responsible for monitoring policy compliance to share information about potential policy violations.

Three Key Areas Need Improvement

Although CMS, HRSA, and the OPTN have taken steps to improve oversight of transplant programs since the high-profile cases came to light, three important areas remain in progress.

• One key unresolved question is the extent to which CMS will conduct on-site reapproval surveys of transplant programs (as part of its new review procedures) after transplant programs gain initial Medicare approval under the new regulations. According to CMS's new regulations, CMS may choose not to conduct on-site reapproval surveys for transplant programs meeting data submission, clinical experience, and outcomes requirements. This means that CMS could potentially choose not to conduct any reapproval surveys for programs meeting these requirements. While CMS officials said that they see value in conducting reapproval surveys, just how CMS will apply its discretion remains unclear. As of January 2008, CMS officials said that the agency had not decided how many reapproval surveys it would conduct or how it would choose which programs to survey among those that meet the aforementioned requirements. They emphasized the agency's need to carefully consider resource constraints in making these decisions. A decision by CMS not to conduct an on-site reapproval survey at a transplant program means that compliance with some CoPs [condition of participation] would not be reviewed unless there was a complaint investigation. As a result, problems at transplant programs unrelated to the data submission, clinical experience, and outcomes requirements—for example, a transplant program failing to provide required protections for living donors or to sufficiently staff its program—could go undetected. In two of the high-profile cases, staffing problems that ultimately affected patients' access to transplants would not have been detected by the outcomes indicator that CMS has now adopted, and the numbers of transplants performed per year at these programs exceeded or were close to CMS's clinical experience requirement.

• Additional questions remain regarding the extent to which CMS will accurately track on-site surveys to avoid the misclassification errors we identified in our review and complete the surveys on a timely basis. As a result of the new transplant regulations, renal transplant programs will no longer share Medicare identification numbers with dialysis facilities, and previously misclassified renal transplant programs will at some point receive a new accurate classification in CMS's survey database once they are approved. However, the potential for transplant programs to be mistakenly classified may remain because transplant programs within the same hospital will share one transplant center Medicare identification number, according to CMS officials. CMS officials said that they were highly aware of the need for their systems to accurately track the status of each transplant program separately. They said that they plan to test for this capability in their new tracking system for transplant programs, which remains under development. What also remains to be seen is the extent to which surveys will occur on a timely basis. Prior to the new regulations, state agencies did not always meet CMS goals for surveying ESRD facilities. Now, under the new regulations, the responsibilities of state agencies that will be conducting on-site surveys of transplant programs will increase, since they will be required to survey both renal and extra-renal transplant programs. With respect to initial approval surveys, CMS's stated plan is that high-priority surveys of transplant programs will be completed by the end of fiscal year 2008, but as of January 2008, CMS officials expressed some uncertainty about meeting this goal. Initial surveys of transplant programs have been given a relatively high priority in the state agency workload, but it is not definite that this high priority level will continue because CMS has revised state agency workload priorities in the past. Further, the priority level for reapproval surveys is not yet known; a lower priority could affect how frequently surveys occur.

• The last unresolved question concerns the OPTN's and HRSA's planned organ acceptance rate indicator, which as part of a set of activity-level indicators, could potentially improve the OPTN's ability to detect transplant programs experiencing problems that prolong the time patients wait for transplants. According to the OPTN, the organ acceptance rate indicator for kidney and liver transplant programs has been developed but, as of February 2008, has not yet been implemented; HRSA officials expect the indicator to be in place within 1 year. HRSA and OPTN officials reported that they are considering developing organ acceptance rate indicators for transplant programs for other organ types. Before extending the indicator to other types of programs, however, the OPTN will first assess the effectiveness of the indicator at detecting potential problems at kidney and liver transplant programs, which perform larger volumes of transplants, and determine the feasibility of developing an indicator for programs with lower transplant volumes, such as heart and lung transplant programs.

Data Should Be Shared

CMS, HRSA, and the OPTN have recognized the importance of sharing data on transplant programs with one another and have taken initial steps to share basic data. To help CMS assess programs' compliance with its new Medicare requirements, the OPTN (through HRSA) is now sending CMS certain basic transplant program data on a quarterly basis. For example, the new Medicare regulations require transplant centers to be OPTN members, so the OPTN is providing data on the status of each transplant center's membership in the OPTN.

While this basic data sharing represents progress, CMS, HRSA, and the OPTN have additional information resulting from their oversight activities that could be shared. The exchange of this information is important because CMS and the

Medicare Requirements for Transplant Programs for Which the OPTN Is Providing Data to CMS

Medicare requirement	Data provided to CMS on each OPTN member
Transplant programs must be a member of the OPTN	OPTN membership status
Transplant programs must submit OPTN-required date to the OPTN within 90 days of OPTN deadlines	Member's compliance with OPTN data submission policies
The hospital in which a transplant program operates must have a written agreement with an organ procurement organization to receive organs	The organ procurement organization with which the transplant center has an agreement
Transplant programs must ensure that all individuals who provide services at the program, supervise services, or both, are qualified to provide or supervise such services	The names of the primary surgeon and primary physician at the transplant program

TAKEN FROM: GAO analysis of Medicare CoPs for transplant centers and information from CMS and HRSA.

OPTN conduct different monitoring activities and, as a result, may have different information about transplant programs that could be relevant to each other. For example, while both CMS and the OPTN conduct on-site reviews of transplant programs, the OPTN's on-site reviews focus largely on medical records review while CMS's on-site surveys are more broadly scoped. If the OPTN determined during an on-site review that the medical urgency assigned to patients by a transplant program was not supported by its medical records, this information could be of interest to CMS if this practice inappropriately reduced the chances of others on the waiting list to receive a transplant. As another example, the OPTN and HRSA are working to put into place their organ acceptance rate indicator, which CMS officials said they would be interested in using. Information from CMS's and the OPTN's investigations could also be potentially important to share. For example, if CMS investigated a complaint from a patient about the length of time he or she had been waiting for a transplant and determined that the delay was caused by the program failing to update the patient's health status, a violation of OPTN policy, the OPTN might want to flag the program for closer monitoring.

CMS and HRSA have recognized the importance of sharing information from their oversight activities, but the agencies have not yet reached agreement on how they would do so. CMS submitted a draft proposal to HRSA in April 2007 describing how CMS and HRSA could potentially share information about organ transplant programs. CMS and HRSA officials have since discussed the initial proposal, including possible revisions, but their progress has been slow. As of February 2008, CMS and HRSA had yet to reach agreement or establish a time frame for doing so. According to HRSA officials it had taken the agencies several months to better understand each other's oversight processes, and both agencies needed to further explore their information needs. CMS officials also indicated that further issues would need to be resolved before an agreement could be reached.

Some Issues Have Not Been Resolved

As part of any agreement to share information from their oversight activities, CMS and HRSA will need to determine precisely what information from their oversight activities they will share and at what point in their oversight processes they will share it. CMS and HRSA have discussed but not resolved these issues:

- *Nature of information to be shared.* It will be important for CMS and HRSA to determine specifically what information they will share from their oversight activities. For example, while CMS's initial proposal addressed how CMS and HRSA could share information from CMS's and the OPTN's investigations of serious complaints, such as those involving threats to patient health and safety, CMS and HRSA officials have since discussed whether to share information from all complaints. In addition, CMS and HRSA have not determined to what extent information from routine inspections, such as the OPTN's on-site reviews and CMS's on-site surveys, will be shared and at what level of detail. For example, CMS's initial proposal called for CMS to notify the OPTN about its completed on-site surveys and to indicate whether the transplant program surveyed had a plan of correction, but it did not call for CMS to provide information on the deficiencies CMS found. HRSA officials have since expressed their interest in having this more detailed information.

- *Timing of information sharing.* A more difficult challenge that CMS and HRSA face is agreeing when to share information about potential problems at transplant programs. Officials from both CMS and HRSA consider the severity of the identified problem(s) with a program to be a key factor in determining the appropriate time for information sharing. In this regard, officials from both agencies stated a willingness to promptly share information on potentially serious problems. Agreeing on just when to exchange information on less serious problems has been more problematic for the agencies in part because of differences in their approaches to oversight. On the one hand, CMS officials emphasize their agency's obligation to investigate any indications of noncompliance with Medicare requirements and prefer to be notified as soon as possible if the OPTN discovers a potential problem indicating noncompliance with Medicare CoPs. On the other hand, HRSA officials have emphasized that the viability and success of the OPTN's performance improvement process depends upon transplant programs sharing openly about their practices or past events. HRSA officials contend that the possibility of such information being shared with CMS, a regulatory agency, could cause transplant programs to be less candid about discussing real or potential problems, making it more difficult for the OPTN to help them return to compliance.

CMS, HRSA, and the OPTN recognize the gaps in oversight that existed when serious problems were exposed at transplant centers and have taken significant steps to strengthen federal oversight. The actions they have taken will help improve standards for transplant programs and should improve detection of potential problems. These actions include CMS's issuance of new regulations that expand and update requirements for transplant programs. In addition, CMS plans to conduct on-site surveys of all transplant programs seeking initial Medicare approval under the new regulations and to regularly review certain transplant program data, which should reduce the chances of problems going undetected by the agency. Similarly, if the OPTN's and HRSA's efforts to develop and implement a set of activity-level indicators to detect problems that prolong the time patients wait for transplants are successful, the indicators will likely result in earlier detection of these more subtle problems.

> "Although bias against transplanting
> people with intellectual disability has
> been reduced, it is still a factor."

The Organ Donation System Remains Biased Against the Disabled

Steven Reiss

The organ donation system is biased against the intellectually disabled, Steven Reiss argues in the following viewpoint. Reiss cites the case of a three-year-old girl with an intellectual disability who was denied a place on a transplant list. While he acknowledges that this prejudice is not as great as it once was, Reiss asserts that it is a sign of the wider problem of access to health care. Reiss is a professor of psychology and psychiatry at Ohio State University.

As you read, consider the following questions:

1. According to the author, how many Americans underwent a liver transplant in 2002?
2. In Reiss's view, what should organ allocation not take into account?

3. What is the solution to saving lives, in the author's opinion?

In 2004 Linda Jones and I started the nation's only formal program on organ transplantation and intellectual disabilities (mental retardation). Linda was a nurse who had retired as head of "Lifeline Ohio," the organ procurement program for central Ohio. I was a professor and head of a university center on intellectual disabilities. In 2002 I underwent liver transplantation at the Ohio State University because an autoimmune disease was destroying my birth liver.

Over the course of three years Linda spoke with many physicians and policy people about the topic. She spoke with people in North America, Europe, and Asia. I hired Marilee Martens to collect data for us for a literature review, which we published in 2006.

Here is what I think about the case of Amelia, the three-year old who has an intellectual disability and was denied listing for a transplant at Children's Hospital in Philadelphia.

The Intellectually Disabled Can Have Successful Transplants

Organ transplantation is as effective with people with intellectual disability as with the general population. It is much more effective than most people realize. I was one of about 16,000 Americans who underwent liver transplant in 2002. A year later more than 90 percent of us were alive.

I think it is likely Children's Hospital will reverse its decision and list Amelia. Huge numbers of people care passionately about this issue. I don't understand what the hospital administrators are waiting for. The longer this goes on, the more will be the damage to the reputation of their hospital.

In the past the system of listing people for transplants and allocating organs had significant bias against people with disabilities, especially those with intellectual disabilities. It was biased against people with certain personality traits and/or mental illness. Clearly, the trend has been toward less bias. People with intellectual disabilities have been successfully transplanted. I don't think the bias has been eliminated but I believe it is greatly reduced from where it was.

Although bias against transplanting people with intellectual disability has been reduced, it is still a factor and needs to be reduced further. Many doctors have expressed such bias to me personally. Many don't share this bias. Freeing the system of bias is a work in progress.

Organ allocation should not take into account disability, personality, or the insurance status of the patient.

If you have a loved one who has an intellectual disability and is denied listing for a transplant by one center, go to another center without delay. The decisions are not the same from one center to another.

A Lack of Health-Care Access Worsens the Problem

The discrimination against people with intellectual disabilities being listed for organ transplants may be part of a larger problem of access to health care, especially for adults. The more Lives Worth Saving looked at transplants, the more we noticed people dying from, say, a cancer that had been diagnosed only a day before death. We heard stories of parents losing their jobs because they had children with special needs posting too many bills with the health insurer.

The United States has a number of federally funded programs in the field of developmental disabilities. Policy makers need to re-direct some of this money and create a national priority on health care for adults with developmental disabilities. My take-away thought from the three years I participated in Lives Worth Saving was, "What is going on with health care for this population? How big must a tumor be before somebody notices it?" I don't think this was about bias. I think it was about access to care.

I believe Amelia's life is worth saving. Nothing in her medical records will change my mind on that point, because it is not a medical judgment. The solution isn't to discover a better way for deciding who gets a kidney and who doesn't. The solution is to find more kidneys.

| *"We need legislation or folks are going to be negative about organ donations."*

Organ Donors Should Consider Where Their Organs End Up

Laura Schlessinger

In the following viewpoint, Laura Schlessinger, also known as Dr. Laura, argues that the organ donation process is unfair and should be more discerning about who receives organ transplants. She believes that potential organ donors should be able to specify categories of people—such as those with a criminal history or substance abuse issues—who may not receive organs from that donor. She further asserts that legislation addressing this issue is needed so that the public will not feel negatively about organ donation. Schlessinger is a radio personality and best-selling author.

As you read, consider the following questions:

1. How many New Yorkers died while waiting for liver transplants as of July 2010, according to data cited by the author?

2. How many people does the author state that Johnny Concepcion passed on New York's transplant waiting list?

3. What recipients would the author like to specify for her organ donations?

As of July, 50 New Yorkers waiting for liver transplants died waiting for an organ, according to the Organ Procurement and Transplant Network.

Johnny Concepcion is not one of them. Concepcion is 42 and a confessed wife killer. He stabbed his wife to death and then drank rat poison in a suicide attempt. The rat poison destroyed his liver so he needed a transplant to survive.

Kerry Sullivan, a fine, upstanding citizen of NYC, has waited a year for a transplanted liver.

The available liver went to . . . Johnny Concepcion—just days after he admitted murdering his wife and destroying his own liver in suicide action.

What?

I remember the furor when a liver transplant was given to Mickey Mantle of baseball fame, when the media revealed that he destroyed his own liver with eons of alcohol abuse.

Obviously, judgment calls have to be made. And they are not supposed to consider religion, gender, financial status, celebrity and so forth—that makes totally fair sense—but really.

Let's go through this again. On July 5, the man murders a woman with 15 stab wounds (after a history of abusing her). Two days later, July 7, he tries to kill himself with rat poison, and he goes immediately to a hospital to get a transplant, passing almost 2,000 people on New York's transplant list and gets an organ and then goes to jail.

I saw a newspaper photo of him in the hospital after the transplant—smiling and giving a V for victory hand signal.

What?

This is a comment from a citizen responding to this news story from the *New York Post*:

> F-d-up World!!! It's funny how they don't put the truth in Commercials for Organ Donation . . . Donate an organ!! Save a Murderer! I have changed my mind on organ donation. I want absolute certainty that my organ goes to someone without criminal history! OR NO THANKS!

I have changed my mind on organ donation. I want absolute certainty that my organ goes to someone without a criminal history—or no thanks.

I believe it is time for people to put caveats on their organ donations: no convicted or confessed murderers, rapists, child molesters, homegrown terrorists, national traitors, long-term alcoholics who destroy their own livers and might likely destroy a new one. . . . We need legislation or folks are going to be negative about organ donations.

If he were to get the death penalty . . . Could we give the liver back to someone he passed on the list?

Just asking.

I am wondering about the dot on my drivers license which indicates me as a potential organ donor. I frankly am going to find out if I can specify that the recipients all be small children. I'll let you know.

> *"Since older candidates on the waiting list are less likely to live long enough to receive a kidney, making them less eligible for transplants will probably result in more deaths on the list."*

How Not to Assign Kidneys

Lainie Friedman Ross and Benjamin E. Hippen

A new proposal to change the way kidneys are allocated could result in more deaths for older patients on the waiting list, Lainie Friedman Ross and Benjamin E. Hippen opine in the following viewpoint. Ross and Hippen argue that the two-pronged system proposed by the United Network for Organ Sharing would result in more deceased-donor kidneys going to patients under the age of fifty, while also reducing the number of live kidney donations. The authors suggest that a more equitable approach would entail expanding living donor transplantations by encouraging kidney swaps and donor chains. Ross is a pediatrician and professor of ethics at the University of Chicago, and Hippen is a transplant nephrologist at the Carolinas Medical Center in Charlotte, North Carolina.

As you read, consider the following questions:

1. How long can deceased-donor kidneys last, as stated by the authors?

2. What is "first-person consent legislation," as explained by Ross and Hippen?

3. According to the authors, what are kidney swaps?

The United Network for Organ Sharing, the nonprofit group that manages the nation's organ transplant system, wants to change the system for allocating kidneys from deceased donors. While organs from living donors are usually directed to a particular person, kidneys from the deceased are distributed under a formula devised by the network. The proposal is supposed to provide deceased-donor kidneys of higher quality to healthier, younger patients instead of to elderly ones who presumably have fewer years to live.

It sounds simple enough. But the strategy could result in fewer kidneys going from living donors to young candidates, and could lead to more deaths of older or sicker candidates on the waiting list. Moreover, it would do nothing to address the fundamental problem: the persistent shortage of kidneys from donors, both living and deceased.

A Two-Pronged Strategy for Kidney Donations

The proposal would set up a two-pronged strategy that is intended to increase the number of life-years gained for every donor kidney. Under the proposal, the top 20 percent of kidneys from deceased donors who had been young and healthy would be assigned to the top 20 percent of young healthy candidates. In other words, the best deceased-donor kidneys would be given to patients likeliest to have long lives ahead of them.

The other 80 percent of deceased-donor kidneys would be allocated first to local candidates within a 15-year age range of the donor, and if no potential candidate were identified, then to the broader pool of candidates. (For example, candidates aged 25 to 55 would get priority for a kidney from a 40-year-old donor who had just died.)

But while the goal is understandable, the proposal is flawed. For one thing, our ability to forecast the success of any particular transplant is limited. The models used to predict whether both the kidney and the recipient survive in any individual operation are correct only 60 percent to 70 percent of the time; sometimes kidneys don't last as long as expected. So basing a vast shift in policy on a model that is just two-thirds accurate should give us pause.

Donations from Living Donors Could Decrease

In addition, giving healthy young patients first dibs on kidneys from young deceased donors might reduce donation rates from living donors to the young candidates, which is at cross-purposes with the goal of extending years of life after transplant. In 2005, the network started giving pediatric transplant candidates priority for kidneys from deceased donors younger than 35. While the pediatric patients received more organs from deceased donors, they got fewer organs from living donors. The likely explanation is that the donors, including many parents, held off, figuring that they could donate later, when the deceased-donor kidney eventually failed. (Those kidneys can last up to 20 years.)

The new proposal would effectively expand the 2005 rule to all healthier, younger candidates, potentially reducing living-donor transplantation to the very group that stands to benefit the most from it. This would only increase their need for another transplant later, since kidneys from deceased donors do not last as long as kidneys from living ones.

Giving more organs to young recipients would also come at the expense of "older" recipients, which in this context can mean 50 to 64. (Only a tiny fraction of all kidneys go to recipients older than 70.) Since older candidates on the waiting list are less likely to live long enough to receive a kidney, making them less eligible for transplants will probably result in more deaths on the list, and more pressure on available living donors to donate to older candidates.

Ways to Reduce the Kidney Shortage

What should be done instead?

First, allocate kidneys on a broader basis. Under both the current and proposed systems, kidneys are allocated locally. But while a New Yorker with end-stage renal disease will typically wait at least six years for a transplant, her counterpart in Minnesota might wait just two to three. Since a kidney from a young deceased donor would probably be allocated to a young local candidate, young candidates in areas with long waiting lists would still be at a substantial disadvantage under the new proposal. Turf disputes among regional and state networks are the main reason geographic disparities haven't been addressed.

Second, the network should continue to support first-person consent legislation under which people who have properly declared their willingness to donate their organs in case of an unexpected death cannot have their wishes overruled by their bereaved families.

But for now, the only sure way to reduce the shortage of organs is to expand transplantation from living donors, which requires more resources from the network. The public needs better education about the benefits of donation by the living and assurances that it is almost always safe. And the network should identify and remove disincentives to donation, like the expenses donors incur for travel or for taking unpaid leave from work for the operation preparation, the procedure and recuperation. We also support tracking the long-term health of living donors, which the network should do more to promote.

The network should also keep encouraging innovative efforts like "kidney swaps" or "donor chains." Kidney swaps involve two donor-recipient pairs who are incompatible within the pair, but can donate to the other pair's recipient. (Think of it as a square dance where the couples switch partners halfway through.)

Donor chains begin with a living donor willing to donate to anyone on the waiting list. Instead of simply giving that donor's kidney to the next patient in line, the kidney can go to the

Fewer Kidneys for Older Patients

The United Network for Organ Sharing (UNOS) is considering a kidney-allocation plant that would give preference to younger patients in an effort to get more life-years from each transplant. Below is how UNOS estimates the new system could affect the percentage of kidney transplants that go to patients in different age groups.

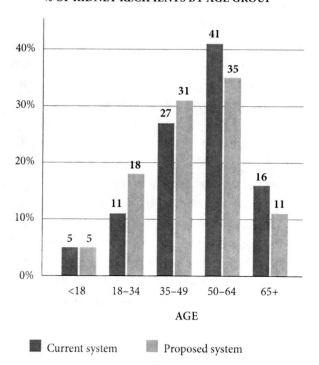

% OF KIDNEY RECIPIENTS BY AGE GROUP

TAKEN FROM: *American Medical News*, "Reallocation Proposition," March 28, 2011.

would-be recipient in an incompatible donor-recipient pair; that donor, in turn, can then give to another recipient of an incompatible donor-recipient pair, with the chain continuing indefinitely. (Consider it the medical equivalent of "pay it forward.")

Patients count on doctors to be not only compassionate in providing care, but also dispassionate in examining data and vigilant in considering the undesirable consequences of any treatment. On these points, the new proposal for allocating kidneys from deceased donors falls short. And on the really pressing issues, it is not nearly ambitious enough.

Periodical and Internet Sources Bibliography

The following articles have been selected to supplement the diverse views presented in this chapter.

Ruth Carol	"Giving Patients a Second Chance at Life," *Minority Nurse*, Winter 2008.
Matthew Cooper and Cynthia L. Forland	"The Elderly as Recipients of Living Donor Kidneys: How Old Is Too Old?," *Current Opinion in Organ Transplantation*, April 2011.
Janice D'Arcy	"Denying an Organ to a 'Mentally Retarded' Child," *Washington Post*, January 17, 2012.
Robert Davis	"More Elderly Having Transplant Surgery," *USA Today*, February 5, 2008.
Charlotte Hays	"Is Denial of Life-Saving Care for Mentally Disabled Girl a Sign of Things to Come?," *National Catholic Register*, February 1, 2012.
Greg A. Knoll	"Is Kidney Transplantation for Everyone?," *Clinical Journal of the American Society of Nephrology*, vol. 4, 2009.
Wayne Kondro	"Plan Proposed to Make Organ Donation Less 'Ad Hoc,'" *Canadian Medical Association Journal*, August 7, 2012.
Danielle Ofri	"When Readiness to Give Can Help Save Your Life," *International Herald Tribune*, February 22, 2012.
Jennifer Wider	"Organ Donation: A Crisis Among Minorities," *JADE*, January–February 2008.
Alan Zarembo	"Dick Cheney: Are Heart Transplants Unusual for Older Patients?," *Los Angeles Times*, March 26, 2012.

OPPOSING
VIEWPOINTS®
SERIES

CHAPTER 2

How Can Organ Donation Be Increased?

Chapter Preface

For parents, few tragedies can be worse than giving birth to an anencephalic infant. Babies born with this condition lack a forebrain and cerebrum; they posses only a brain stem, which allows for autonomic functions such as breathing and sucking. However, without the higher-level brain functions, death is inevitable and typically occurs within days, if not hours. The desire of some families to find meaning in this tragedy has led to a debate on whether anencephalic infants should become organ donors. The issue is one that is both morally and medically complicated.

The primary issue facing the use of anencephalic newborns as organ donors is that they are not technically brain dead—the standard criterion used to determine whether someone can donate organs. Typically, by the time one of these infants is considered brain dead, their organs have deteriorated too much to be of use. Redefining brain death for anencephalic newborns would be one way to increase the size of the donor pool. Fazal Khan and Brian Lea, in an article in the *Indiana Health Law Review*, suggest classifying these infants as "'brain-absent' to a degree sufficient to justify their treatment as brain dead." Khan and Lea argue that this reclassification recognizes that newborns with anencephaly are very similar to brain-dead individuals. The authors conclude: "Allowing donation of organs from anencephalic infants seems proper as it benefits the recipients of the organs and the families of both the donor and recipient, while burdening the anencephalic donor herself to little or no degree." The Florida Pediatric Society's Commission on Bioethics concurs, suggesting that pediatricians ought to advocate for parents who want to donate their infant's organs.

However, there are also arguments against anencephalic organ donations from both a medical and religious perspective. In contrast to the Florida society, the Canadian Paediatric Society (CPS) opposes anencephalic donation. According to a position paper by the CPS, allowing this type of organ donation could result in "application of similar arguments in favour of organ donation from other seriously brain-damaged living patients [and] serious risk of loss of public trust in transplantation programs." In the view of the organization Catholics United for the Faith, anencephalic donation is not just an issue of medical ethics but morality as well. The organization contends, "Removing the organs of an anencephalic infant, even if it is doubtfully human conceptus, includes the willingness to destroy it even if it is human, and thus, incurs the moral malice of murder."

There are more people in the United States that need organs than there are organs available, and finding ways to bridge that gap can be very controversial, as shown in the debate over using anencephalic infants as organ donors. In the following chapter, authors evaluate ways to increase organ donation.

> "The truly decent route would be to allow people to withhold or give their organs freely, especially upon death, even if in exchange for money."

The Selling of Organs Should Be Legalized

Anthony Gregory

In the following viewpoint, Anthony Gregory argues that the creation of a legal organ market would help solve the transplant organ shortage in the United States. He asserts that the health of a kidney donor is not harmed by the donation, and that self-ownership should include the right to sell one's organs. He believes that a legal and legitimate market will rectify the negative and criminal aspects of the organ trade, such as the exploitation of donors. Anthony Gregory is a research editor at the Independent Institute, a libertarian think tank based in California.

As you read, consider the following questions:

1. How many people died in 2008 while waiting for a kidney transplant, according to the viewpoint?
2. How did Iran solve its kidney shortage, as explained by the author?

Anthony Gregory, "Why Legalizing Organ Sales Would Help to Save Lives, End Violence," *The Atlantic*, November 9, 2011. Copyright © 2011 by The Independent Institute. All rights reserved. Reproduced by permission.

3. According to the World Health Organization, as cited by Gregory, the black market accounts for what percent of kidney transplants worldwide?

Last month, New Yorker Levy Izhak Rosenbaum pled guilty in federal court to the crime of facilitating illegal kidney transplants. It has been deemed the first proven case of black market organ trafficking in the United States. His lawyers argue that his lawbreaking was benevolent: "The transplants were successful and the donors and recipients are now leading full and healthy lives."

Indeed, why are organ sales illegal? Donors of blood, semen, and eggs, and volunteers for medical trials, are often compensated. Why not apply the same principle to organs?

The very idea of legalization might sound gruesome to most people, but it shouldn't, especially since research shows it would save lives. In the United States, where the 1984 National Organ Transplantation Act prohibits compensation for organ donating, there are only about 20,000 kidneys every year for the approximately 80,000 patients on the waiting list. In 2008, nearly 5,000 died waiting.

A global perspective shows how big the problem is. "Millions of people suffer from kidney disease, but in 2007 there were just 64,606 kidney-transplant operations in the entire world," according to George Mason University professor and Independent Institute research director Alexander Tabarrok, writing in the *Wall Street Journal*.

A Legal Market Can End Organ Shortages

Almost every other country has prohibitions like America's. In Iran, however, selling one's kidney for profit is legal. There are no patients anguishing on the waiting list. The Iranians have solved their kidney shortage by legalizing sales.

Many will protest that an organ market will lead to exploitation and unfair advantages for the rich and powerful. But these

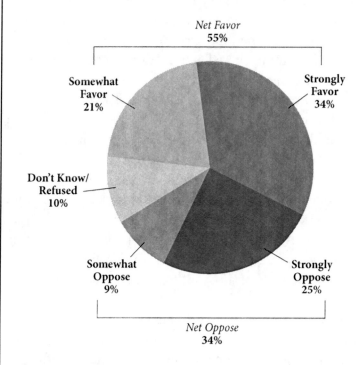

Fifty-Five Percent of the Public Supports an Organ Market

Would you favor or oppose allowing healthy people under medical supervision to sell their organs to patients who need them for transplants?

Net Favor
55%

Somewhat
Favor
21%

Strongly
Favor
34%

Don't Know/
Refused
10%

Somewhat
Oppose
9%

Strongly
Oppose
25%

Net Oppose
34%

TAKEN FROM: Reason Foundation, Reason-Rupe Public Opinion Research Project, March 2012 Questionnaire. http://reason.com/poll.

are the characteristics of the current illicit organ trade. Moreover, as with drug prohibition today and alcohol prohibition in the 1920s, pushing a market underground is the way to make it rife with violence and criminality.

In Japan, for the right price, you can buy livers and kidneys harvested from executed Chinese prisoners. Three years ago in India, police broke up an organ ring that had taken as many as 500 kidneys from poor laborers. The World Health

Organization estimates that the black market accounts for 20 percent of kidney transplants worldwide. Everywhere from Latin America to the former Soviet Republics, from the Philippines to South Africa, a huge network has emerged typified by threats, coercion, intimidation, extortion, and shoddy surgeries.

Although not every black market transaction is exploitative—demonstrating that organ sales, in and of themselves, are not the problem—the most unsavory parts of the trade can be attributed to the fact that it is illegal. Witnessing the horror stories, many are calling on governments to crack down even more severely. Unfortunately, prohibition drives up black-market profits, turns the market over to organized crime, and isolates those harmed in the trade from the normal routes of recourse.

Several years ago, transplant surgeon Nadley Hakim at St. Mary's Hospital in London pointed out that "this trade is going on anyway, why not have a controlled trade where if someone wants to donate a kidney for a particular price, that would be acceptable? If it is done safely, the donor will not suffer."

Bringing the market into the open is the best way to ensure the trade's appropriate activity. Since the stakes would be very high, market forces and social pressure would ensure that people are not intimidated or defrauded. In the United States, attitudes are not so casual as to allow gross degeneracy. Enabling a process by which consenting people engage in open transactions would mitigate the exploitation of innocent citizens and underhanded dealing by those seeking to skirt the law.

Organ Sales Are Consistent with the Ideals of Civil Liberty and Free Markets

The most fundamental case for legalizing organ sales—an appeal to civil liberty—has proven highly controversial. Liberals like to say, "my body, my choice," and conservatives claim to favor free markets, but true self-ownership would include the right to sell one's body parts, and genuine free enterprise would imply a market in human organs. In any event, studies show that this has become a matter of life and death.

Perhaps the key to progress is more widespread exposure to the facts. In 2008, six experts took on this issue [in] an Oxford-style debate hosted by National Public Radio. By the end, those in the audience who favored allowing the market climbed from 44 to 60 percent.

Yet, the organ trade continues to operate in the shadows and questionable activities occur in the medical establishment under the color of law. Even today, doctors sometimes legally harvest organ tissue from dead patients without consent. Meanwhile, thousands are perishing and even more are suffering while we wait for the system to change.

The truly decent route would be to allow people to withhold or give their organs freely, especially upon death, even if in exchange for money. Thousands of lives would be saved. Once again, humanitarianism is best served by the respect for civil liberty, and yet we are deprived both, with horribly unfortunate consequences, just to maintain the pretense of state-enforced propriety.

| "*Many doctors worry that paying for organs is too dangerous a path.*"

Tax Cuts for Organs?

Priya Shetty

In the following viewpoint, Priya Shetty argues that offering people financial incentives, such as tax cuts or free health insurance, in exchange for donating their kidney or portion of their lung, pancreas, or liver, could cause potential ethical problems. According to Shetty, poor people could risk being exploited by an incentive system, while a black market could also emerge. Shetty suggests that another option might be to introduce a system of presumed consent but also notes that might introduce its own set of problems. Shetty is a science journalist whose work has appeared in The Lancet *and the* Guardian.

As you read, consider the following questions:

1. In what year did the United States ban the sale of organs, as stated by Shetty?
2. Why does Benjamin Hippen think poor people would not be ideal organ donors, as explained by the author?
3. As stated by the author, what proportion of donated kidneys is from the black market?

Priya Shetty, "Tax Cuts for Organs?," *The Lancet*, vol. 374, October 17, 2009, pp. 1315–1316. Copyright © 2009 by Elsevier. All rights reserved. Reproduced by permission.

Sally Satel is one of the lucky ones. After being diagnosed with kidney failure in 2004, and facing years of dialysis, she was offered a kidney by someone she barely knew. She had already had a few heartbreaking near-misses with friends offering their kidney, only to later retract the offer. She finally had a transplant in 2006, when a journalist acquaintance made good on her offer to donate.

Satel, a psychiatrist at the Oasis Clinic, Washington, DC, and lecturer at the Yale University School of Medicine, New Haven, CT, USA, realises that she could easily have become one of the thousands dying on waiting lists because of the severe organ shortage.

Although buying and selling organs is still illegal in most countries, including the USA, a controversial proposal to reduce organ shortages by offering donors a financial incentive has been gaining ground with advocates like Satel. With the demand for organs far rapidly outstripping supply, it is a compelling argument, but many doctors worry that paying for organs is too dangerous a path.

In 1984, the US National Organ Transplant Act banned the sale of organs. Although living donors can donate a portion of their liver, lung, or pancreas, the need for kidneys is by far the highest. This year, over 100,000 people in the USA are waiting for an organ, of whom about 80,000 need a kidney. According to the United Network on Organ Sharing, based in the USA, which manages organ procurement and transplants on behalf of the government, between January and September there have only been another 7,000 donors.

As the crisis in the supply of organs worsens, some transplant surgeons are calling for a radical effort to increase donations by offering substantial financial rewards in exchange for organs. There is some precedent for the commercialisation of human body parts. For instance, women help other women conceive by selling their eggs or acting as paid surrogates. This June , the state of New York made it legal for women to be paid for donating eggs for research.

The incentives proposed for organ donors are substantial tax cuts, free lifetime health insurance, or free college tuition. Cash could be included too, although Satel says it could appeal to people who are desperate for quick money such as those with large gambling debts. Donors do incur some costs (panel) and even those who oppose incentives, such as the US National Kidney Foundation, agree that compensating donors for loss of earnings or paying for donation-related health-care insurance costs is fair.

But the idea of financially motivating donors to give organs is anathema to many doctors. "Donors are human beings, they are not pigs on a farm", says Gabriel Danovitch, director of the kidney transplant programme at the University of California, Los Angeles, CA, USA. Arthur Caplan, director of the University of Pennsylvania's Center for Bioethics, PA, USA, agrees. "Paying people to maim themselves for money is a violation of the do no harm ethic of medicine", he says.

International organisations are also yet to be convinced. WHO and the World Medical Association have ruled against payments to donors. Last year, the Istanbul Declaration, which was signed by 77 countries in an effort to eliminate organ trafficking and transplant tourism (when people from high-income countries travel to low-income countries to procure organs), also ruled against the commercialisation of living donations. And a European Union resolution last year said that any payment should be confined "solely to compensation strictly limited to making good the expense and inconvenience associated with the donation".

One concern is the potential for exploiting the poor. Even non-cash benefits could be valuable enough (e.g., free health care in the USA) to hold a powerful appeal for the least well off. But Benjamin Hippen, a nephrologist at Metrolina Nephrology Associates based in Charlotte, NC, USA, says that extremely poor people would not be ideal donors in any case because "low socioeconomic status around the world is an independent risk factor for kidney disease. In the long term, the recipient may not be better off with a kidney from someone at high risk, and the donor themselves might develop kidney failure".

The overriding concern among critics of the proposal, however, is the danger a US organ market could unleash. A special issue of *Current Opinions on Organ Transplantation* highlighted concerns about the organ trade in developing countries. In one paper, Ejaz Ahmed, at the Sindh Institute of Urology, and colleagues say that in Pakistan, the poor are heavily exploited—in 2007, over 70% of the 2,500 kidney transplants came from the extremely poor. In the same issue, Benita Padilla, at the National Kidney and Transplant Institute in the Philippines, argued for legislation against transplant commercialism for similar reasons.

The shortage of organs means that trafficking has skyrocketed—WHO estimates that a fifth of the 70,000 kidneys transplanted around the world every year are from the black market. Hippen argues that paying donors in the USA could eliminate organ trafficking. "What provides the economic support [for trafficking] is wealthy people from North America and western Europe".

Iran is the only country that has any semblance of a regulated paid donor system, but Ahmed's team say the country has seen deceased donations plummet as a result. And, although Iran has theoretically outlawed transplant tourism, "that isn't quite the case in reality", says Francis Delmonico, professor of surgery at Harvard Medical School, Boston, MA, USA.

Advocates of financial incentives argue that a US market would be saved by regulation. Caplan disagrees, saying that "given the failure to regulate the mortgage industry, savings and loans, banking, and stock markets in nearly every nation why would anyone think a kidney market could be regulated?" Delmonico also thinks black markets are inevitable. "Once you say it's okay to have a market, you won't be able to fix a price and ensure that price is the only game in town". Crucially, if the law were changed to allow financial incentives, there would be no going back if it

Tax Incentives for Organ Donors Would Prevent Low-Income Donors from Profiting

While there are contexts in which paternalism may be justified ... [tax incentives are] not one of them because it involves adults who are fully competent to enter into contracts. Indeed, financial decisions as to cadaveric donations are significantly less risky and harmful than countless other decisions the law permits competent adults to make each day—for example, to drink alcohol, scuba dive, or work in a coal mine or on construction projects. Put another way, if we are going to commercialize human bodies by providing financial incentives for harvesting organs, those incentives should be available to all who qualify based on relevant factors (like health) and not based on an individual's tax bracket. Our bodies are uniquely ours, and preventing low income persons from profiting because we do not believe they can make as free and as informed of a choice as middle or high income persons is paternalistic and demeaning.

Lisa Milot, "The Case Against Tax Incentives for Organ Transfers," Willamette Law Review, *vol. 45, Fall 2008.*

did not work, says Danovitch. "It would be like putting an egg back together after you've cracked it".

The American Medical Association has been pushing for pilot studies to gauge whether financial incentives would work in practice, although none have yet been started. Until major organisations get behind the concept, it seems unlikely that incentives will be introduced. However, Mark Cherry, professor of philosophy at Saint Edward's University in Austin, TX, USA, says that although no big organisation has yet come out in favour, transplant surgeons have admitted to him in private that they support incentives. He believes they do not go public with their views for fear of professional vilification.

One way to boost the organ supply could be a system of presumed consent, where everyone is considered a potential donor unless they opt out. The idea has political backing in the USA. In September, Cass Sunstein, Barack Obama's nominee to head the Office of Information and Regulatory Affairs, came out strongly in favour of it. But the system has had mixed results in Europe. Spain, which introduced presumed consent in 1990 has seen donations double, but Sweden saw hardly any increase in donation rates.

The notion that organs "belong to the state" after death is difficult to enforce in the face of grieving family members who do not want to give consent, says Hippen. Pressing the issue is likely to undermine trust in the medical profession, he says.

The UK decided last year not to introduce presumed consent for this very reason. It plans to focus instead on recruiting extra donor transplant coordinators and 24-h organ retrieval teams—factors that some believe explain Spain's high donor rates.

Presumed consent "is a way of the government taxing even your body parts, which strikes me as horrific and coercive", says Cherry. He would prefer "organ futures", where a person agrees that their organs can be sold after death. This approach could be especially useful for heart and lung transplants, says Robert Sade, head of the Medical University of South Carolina, Charleston, SC, USA. "Cash contributions to the estates of deceased donors, substantial tax benefits, or payment of funeral expenses might clear those waiting lists", he says.

Meanwhile, the severe organ shortage seems to have already created a black market in the USA. Earlier this year, the Federal Bureau of Investigation (FBI) arrested a group of fraudulent politicians and rabbis, one of whom allegedly bought a kidney from an impoverished Israeli for US$10,000, and tried to sell it for $160,000.

This revelation did not surprise Satel. The waiting list for a kidney can be as long as 10 years, which is longer than people who need one are likely to live. "Everyone was so shocked [by the FBI's discovery], but do people really think we are going to sit by and die?" she asks.

The desperation Satel speaks of is felt by many on waiting lists. On Sept 13, the Irish screenwriter Frank Deasy wrote of the trauma of waiting for an organ in the UK newspaper *The Observer*. "Whole families are living on the list", he wrote, "struggling to carry on normal life, their hopes and dreams, their children's futures, in the balance". Deasy died 4 days later, when the long-awaited transplant materialised, but failed to save him.

> *"Presumed consent, financial compensation for living and deceased donors and point systems would all increase the supply of transplant organs."*

The Meat Market

Alex Tabarrok

In the following viewpoint, Alex Tabarrok contends that one way to reduce the organ shortage in the United States is by following the lead of countries such as Singapore and adopting a policy of pre-sumed consent. He explains that under presumed consent everyone is a potential organ donor unless they opt out. According to Tabarrok, countries with presumed consent laws have seen modest in-creases in organ donations. Tabarrok further argues that financial compensation and point systems that give potential organ donors higher placement on organ waiting lists would also help solve the shortage. Tabarrok is a professor of economics at George Mason University.

As you read, consider the following questions:

1. What is cardiac death, as defined by the author?

2. In Tabarrok's opinion, what do the Iranian donation system and the black market demonstrate?

3. What is "no give, no take," as explained by the author?

Harvesting human organs for sale! The idea suggests the lurid world of horror movies and 19th-century grave robbers. Yet right now, Singapore is preparing to pay donors as much as 50,000 Singapore dollars (almost US$36,000) for their organs. Iran has eliminated waiting lists for kidneys entirely by paying its citizens to donate. Israel is implementing a "no give, no take" system that puts people who opt out of the donor system at the bottom of the transplant waiting list should they ever need an organ.

Millions of people suffer from kidney disease, but in 2007 there were just 64,606 kidney-transplant operations in the entire world. In the U.S. alone, 83,000 people wait on the official kidney-transplant list. But just 16,500 people received a kidney transplant in 2008, while almost 5,000 died waiting for one.

To combat yet another shortfall, some American doctors are routinely removing pieces of tissue from deceased patients for transplant without their, or their families', prior consent. And the practice is perfectly legal. In a number of U.S. states, medical examiners conducting autopsies may and do harvest corneas with little or no family notification. (By the time of autopsy, it is too late to harvest organs such as kidneys.) Few people know about routine removal statutes and perhaps because of this, these laws have effectively increased cornea transplants.

Routine removal is perhaps the most extreme response to the devastating shortage of organs world-wide. That shortage is leading some countries to try unusual new methods to increase donation. Innovation has occurred in the U.S. as well, but progress has been slow and not without cost or controversy.

Organs can be taken from deceased donors only after they have been declared dead, but where is the line between life and death? Philosophers have been debating the dividing line between baldness and nonbaldness for over 2,000 years, so there is little hope that the dividing line between life and death will ever be agreed upon. Indeed, the great paradox of deceased donation is that we must draw the line between life and death precisely where we cannot be sure of the answer, because the line must lie where the donor is dead but the donor's organs are not.

In 1968 the *Journal of the American Medical Association* published its criteria for brain death. But reduced crime and better automobile safety have led to fewer potential brain-dead donors than in the past. Now, greater attention is being given to donation after cardiac death: no heart beat for two to five minutes (protocols differ) after the heart stops beating spontaneously. Both standards are controversial—the surgeon who performed the first heart transplant from a brain-dead donor in 1968 was threatened with prosecution, as have been some surgeons using donation after cardiac death. Despite the controversy, donation after cardiac death more than tripled between 2002 and 2006, when it accounted for about 8% of all deceased donors nationwide. In some regions, that figure is up to 20%.

The shortage of organs has increased the use of so-called expanded-criteria organs, or organs that used to be considered unsuitable for transplant. Kidneys donated from people over the age of 60 or from people who had various medical problems are more likely to fail than organs from younger, healthier donors, but they are now being used under the pressure. At the University of Maryland's School of Medicine five patients recently received transplants of kidneys that had either cancerous or benign tumors removed from them. Why would anyone risk cancer? Head surgeon Dr. Michael Phelan explained, "the ongoing shortage of organs from deceased donors, and the high risk of dying while waiting for a transplant, prompted five donors and recipients to push ahead with surgery." Expanded-criteria organs are a useful response to the shortage, but their use also means that the shortage is even worse than it appears

inequality in kidney allocation. Moreover, this proposal would save the government money since even with a significant payment, transplant is cheaper than the dialysis that is now paid for by Medicare's End Stage Renal Disease program.

In March 2009 Singapore legalized a government plan for paying organ donors. Although it's not clear yet when this will be implemented, the amounts being discussed for payment, around $50,000, suggest the possibility of a significant donor incentive. So far, the U.S. has lagged other countries in addressing the shortage, but last year, Sen. Arlen Specter circulated a draft bill that would allow U.S. government entities to test compensation programs for organ donation. These programs would only offer noncash compensation such as funeral expenses for deceased donors and health and life insurance or tax credits for living donors.

World-wide we will soon harvest more kidneys from living donors than from deceased donors. In one sense, this is a great success—the body can function perfectly well with one kidney so with proper care, kidney donation is a low-risk procedure. In another sense, it's an ugly failure. Why must we harvest kidneys from the living, when kidneys that could save lives are routinely being buried and burned? A payment of funeral expenses for the gift of life or a discount on driver's license fees for those who sign their organ donor card could increase the supply of organs from deceased donors, saving lives and also alleviating some of the necessity for living donors.

Two countries, Singapore and Israel, have pioneered nonmonetary incentives systems for potential organ donors. In Singapore anyone may opt out of its presumed consent system. However, those who opt out are assigned a lower priority on the transplant waiting list should they one day need an organ, a system I have called "no give, no take."

Many people find the idea of paying for organs repugnant but they do accept the ethical foundation of no give, no take— that those who are willing to give should be the first to receive.

In addition to satisfying ethical constraints, no give, no take increases the incentive to sign one's organ donor card thereby reducing the shortage. In the U.S., Lifesharers.org, a nonprofit network of potential organ donors (for which I am an adviser), is working to implement a similar system.

In Israel a more flexible version of no give, no take will be phased into place beginning this year. In the Israeli system, people who sign their organ donor cards are given points pushing them up the transplant list should they one day need a transplant. Points will also be given to transplant candidates whose first-degree relatives have signed their organ donor cards or whose first-degree relatives were organ donors. In the case of kidneys, for example, two points (on a 0- to 18-point scale) will be given if the candidate had three or more years previous to being listed signed their organ card. One point will be given if a first-degree relative has signed and 3.5 points if a first-degree relative has previously donated an organ.

The world-wide shortage of organs is going to get worse before it gets better, but we do have options. Presumed consent, financial compensation for living and deceased donors and point systems would all increase the supply of transplant organs. Too many people have died already but pressure is mounting for innovation that will save lives.

> "'Presumed consent' proposals such
> as Colorado's . . . actually reduce the
> overall number of available organs."

Presumed Consent Is the Wrong Way to Increase Organ Donation

Daniel Sayani

A proposed law in Colorado that would presume all Coloradans with a driver's license or ID card have consented to become organ donors is a threat to individual liberty, Daniel Sayani argues in the following viewpoint. According to Sayani, the legislation ignores individuals' rights to bodily autonomy and could result in doctors viewing patients as potential sources of organs, rather than lives worthy of being saved. He also argues that presumed consent will not solve the organ shortage, and most Coloradans are willing to donate organs without being coerced. Sayani is a contributor to The New American *magazine.*

As you read, consider the following questions:

1. According to Sayani, from where do Colorado legislators believe bodily freedom stems?

2. What was the conclusion of a study conducted in the Netherlands, as cited by Sayani?

3. What proportion of Coloradans has voluntarily expressed interest in organ donation, as stated by the author?

Some Colorado state legislators are proposing to make theirs the first state in which people become organ donors by default. The proposal, introduced in the state Senate last week [January 2011], would change the process for renewing driver's licenses and ID cards so applicants are assumed to be organ and tissue donors unless they initial a statement saying they want to opt out, according to the *Huffington Post*.

Entitled "A Bill Concerning Presumed Consent for Organ and Tissue Donation," SB 11-042 was introduced in the General Assembly by Democrat State Representative Dan Pabon, and initially was supported by Democrat State Senator Lucia Guzman. Guzman, however, last night declared that she has changed her mind. The *Washington Post* reports:

> Democratic Sen. Lucia Guzman told Denver's KUSA-TV that she is dropping her proposal that the state change to a "presumed consent" system.
>
> That system automatically classifies all applicants for driver's licenses and state ID cards as organ and tissue donors unless they opt out. Such donations are used in several European countries but have raised ethical concerns in the US.

The Colorado proposal was introduced last week and sparked fears and opposition from many. According to the text of the legislation:

> The bill changes the organ donation program so that a person is presumed to have consented to organ and tissue donation at the time the person applies for or renews a driver's license or identification card unless the person initials a statement that

states that the person does not want to be considered as a possible organ and tissue donor.

The text of the bill amends driver's license and photo ID renewal forms to read:

> You are automatically deemed to have consented to being an organ and tissue donor and this designation will appear on your driver's license or identification card.

Giving Up Bodily Autonomy

The legislation makes no explicit exemptions or provisions stating that if individuals die prior to being able to sign or initial the state-run DMV form, their organs will be protected from state-sanctioned organ harvesting, even if it violates their ethical or religious beliefs, or their dying wishes to not donate organs.

The state mistakenly assumes that unless individuals initial the specific document provided by the Department of Motor Vehicles, they are expressing their desire to donate organs and living tissue, resting on the fallacious notion that "silence equals (or implies) consent." Colorado wants its citizens to effectively surrender their bodily autonomy to the state if they fail to sign a state-sanctioned document.

The proposal is a revelatory example of positivism. The individual's right to bodily autonomy is not a factor at play in the minds of the bill's sponsors; instead, they do not view the individual's right to control his own body as existing from Natural Law or from God, believing rather that state-issued documentation from the Department of Motor Vehicles is the only binding, admissible, and significant element at play in the corporal freedoms of the governed.

In other words, to these legislators, one's bodily freedom stems not from God, but from the Colorado DMV—and not even one's own organs are safe from the clutches of the state.

The Colorado proposal is yet another example of an Orwellian [reminiscent of George Orwell's works depicting an authoritarian state] assault on individual liberty, including religious liberty and patients' rights. It also indicates a step in the direction of the overall aim of so-called "Healthcare Reform": the inevitable slump toward rationing care and sacrificing the individual's access to life-saving treatments and services in the interest of the "greater good of others."

People are essentially being threatened with becoming organ donors against their wishes. Bioethicists and health policy experts have warned that if doctors view all patients as prospective donors, they will no longer consider them as patients worthy of having their lives prolonged, but instead will see them as walking organ banks—mere commodities that fulfill the utilitarian function of providing organs to others.

Once again, government is acting contrary to the fundamental Lockean (referring to the philosopher John Locke) notion that the individual is the effective owner of his body, and has the right to determine what he will do with it (while acknowledging that God, as Creator, is ultimately in control of the body, and prohibits individuals from doing anything contrary to self-preservation, according to John Locke's *Second Treatise on Government*).

Presumed Consent Is Ineffective

"Presumed consent" proposals such as Colorado's, widely considered by experts to be unethical, actually *reduce* the overall number of available organs, as individuals are less likely to volunteer as donors when they are aware of such coercive Orwellian policies as state-sanctioned organ harvesting.

According to an article in the *British Medical Journal* by Linda Wright, Director of Bioethics for the Toronto-based University Health Network, and Assistant Professor of Surgery at the University of Toronto Medical School, presumed consent is also ineffective at ameliorating the plight of those on waiting lists for organ transplants. She notes:

Research indicates that Presumed Consent will not answer the organ shortage. It has not eliminated waiting lists despite evidence that it increased organ donation in some countries.

Wright's argument also posits that efforts to utilize "presumed consent" as a quick fix to the nation's organ shortage are merely superficial and neglect to address the root causes of the shortage. As summarized by the *New York Times*:

> She also says encouraging people to talk to their families about their wishes on donation, engaging communities to help build the necessary trust to favor organ donation, and increasing our knowledge of what influences donation rates are also important. Finally, meeting the demand for organs may require not only increasing organ supply but also optimizing disease prevention and recipient selection, she adds. "Given the multi-factorial nature of the problem, presumed consent alone will not solve the organ shortage," she concludes.

A [2005] study conducted in the Netherlands, published in the journal *Transplant International* examined whether different consent systems explain the difference in organ donation rates among countries when taking into account the difference in relevant mortality rates. Researchers, who analyzed data on donation and relevant mortality rates for 10 different countries as well as information on the existing consent systems, concluded,

> International comparative legal research has shown that the differences between decision systems are marginal. When the national organ donation rates are corrected for mortality rates, these findings are confirmed: the donor efficiency rate shows that opting-out systems do not automatically guarantee higher donation rates than opting-in systems.

Organ Transplants Are a Gift

Informed consent respects and acknowledges the essential formality of the transplanted organ as a *gift* that one person gives to another. A necessary dimension of a gift as gift is that it must be given. It must be endowed; one cannot receive a gift from the other if the other has not consented to the giving. In effect, without the giver's consent, the so-called gift has been taken rather than been received. . . . Without informed consent, a transplanted organ ceases to be a gift; it is something taken. Some may even say that it is something stolen.

Nicanor Austriaco, "Presumed Consent for Organ Procurement," National Catholic Bioethics Quarterly, *Summer 2009.*

Consent Must Be Voluntary

Agreeing with the professional opinion of Wright is virologist Gee Yen Shin, who authored an editorial entitled "Presumed Consent is too Paternalistic," in which he wrote that while presumed consent is an "attractive utilitarian approach to solving a perennial dilemma," it is nonetheless unethical. He continued:

> What of the autonomy of individuals and patients? Is it acceptable or just to presume that the sick and the dying are content to surrender their organs after death? I believe that government, "the State," exists to serve the people, not the other way around. Harvesting organs from citizens who have died on the basis of presumed consent is the most macabre manifestation of the latter that one could imagine.
>
> Given the shortage of organs in the UK, the preoccupation with the preservation of patient autonomy may seem

dogmatic and possibly eccentric, but this inconvenient concept underpins the ethics behind modern medical practice. The State brushes autonomy and free will aside at its peril. If the Government goes ahead with presumed consent for organ donation, it will irrevocably alter the relationship between the State and its citizens.

Philosopher Hugh McLachlan is also of the opinion that presumed consent is:

> . . . a very troublesome notion. Consent must be voluntarily and knowingly expressed in order to serve the function of morally authorizing actions of other people towards and concerning the consenting person that otherwise would be morally wrong. To say that it can reasonably be presumed that we consent to donate our organs if we do not specifically say that we do not consent is absurd. It is a deceitful piece of sophistry.

Similar Legislation Has Been Rejected

The proposed legislation is also suspect because Colorado already has one of the highest organ donation rates of any state in the country. According to the Colorado Donor Alliance, over two-thirds of Coloradans have already expressed their voluntary desire to donate organs on driver's licenses and identification cards, and as a result, the organization, Colorado's premier advocacy group for organ donation, opposes the legislation. According to Sue Dunn, President and CEO of the Donor Alliance, the legislation may even reduce the number of organ donors:

> I don't think it should pass right now. And that is an awkward [thing] for me to say running an organ and tissue recovery agency. What we don't know and what has not been shown in any state in the country, is will rates go up or down. Would the way that it gets presented at the driver's license office actually increase the number of people who say no?

Such legislative efforts have also been proposed by Democrats in New York and Delaware, and have soundly been rejected in both states. In New York, the Catholic League for Civil and Religious Rights and the Orthodox Jewish groups Agudath Israel of America and the Rabbinical Alliance of America effectively lobbied for the bill's defeat—a victory for the Lockean principle of corporal liberty.

New York Assemblyman Dov Hikind expressed fear that such bills result in "protracted legal battles over organ harvesting," and Professor McLachlan seconds this claim, arguing that "presumed consent" paves a path for organ harvesting as an "opt-out" system.

In light of State Senator Guzman's withdrawal from supporting the Colorado bill, its fate remains uncertain. [Editor's Note: In February 2011, Colorado's Senate Committee on Health and Human Services voted to postpone the bill indefinitely.] Colorado's Republican State Senator Shawn Mitchell says,

> If enough people aren't volunteering, that doesn't mean the government can suddenly lay claim to their body and to their organs after they die. People, I would hope, would be willing to make this choice, but if they're not, the government doesn't own their bodies. They do and after they're dead, their families do.

Those who believe in the religious and ethical liberties of human beings, as well as in public health decisions that are empirically and ethically validated, will continue to stand firm against "presumed consent" efforts.

Periodical and Internet Sources Bibliography

The following articles have been selected to supplement the diverse views presented in this chapter.

Ted Alcorn	"China's Organ Transplant System in Transition," *The Lancet*, June 4, 2011.
Nicanor Pier Giorgio Austriaco	"Presumed Consent for Organ Procurement," *National Catholic Bioethics Quarterly*, Summer 2009.
Alexander Berger	"Why Selling Organs Should Be Legal," *New York Times*, December 5, 2011.
Sarah Boehm	"Presumed Consent: A Bad Thing," *British Medical Journal*, February 16, 2008.
The Economist	"Opting Out of Opting Out," November 20, 2008.
The Economist	"The Gap Between Supply and Demand," October 9, 2008.
Benjamin Hippen and Arthur Matas	"The Point of Control: Can a Regulated Organ Market Be Moral?," *Hastings Center Report*, November–December 2009.
Ana Lita	"The Dark Side of Organ Transplantation," *The Humanist*, March–April 2008.
David Schwark	"Organ Conscription: How the Dead Can Save the Living," *Journal of Law and Health*, Summer 2011.
Wesley J. Smith	"Presumptuous Consent," *First Things*, May 18, 2010.

What Ethical Issues Surround Organ Donation?

Chapter Preface

Like many medical issues, organ donation has a set of ethical complications. One of the biggest ethical controversies in organ donation involves China. Each year, approximately 1.5 million people in China are in need of transplants. However, only ten thousand of those people undergo the procedure, in part because the cadaver organ donation rate is one of the world's lowest, at a mere 0.03 per 1 million people. In the past, the Chinese government has sought to close this gap by harvesting organs from executed prisoners, a policy that has garnered widespread criticism. However, the government vowed in March 2012 to stop that practice by 2017 and focus its efforts on building a voluntary organ donation system. Despite that major change, organ donation in China is likely to remain ethically complex.

One challenge facing China is Confucian views on organ donation. Confucianism, which can be considered both a philosophy and a religion, opposes organ donation based on the view that the body should remain intact from birth through burial. Li Li, writing for the weekly newsmagazine *Beijing Review*, explains: "Chinese customs call for people to be buried or cremated with the body intact. One die-hard superstition has it that if an organ is taken from a body after death, the person in question will be reborn with a handicap in that organ in his or her next life." However, in 2000, South Korea, another nation in which Confucianism predominates, formally recognized brain death for the purposes of organ donation, so it is possible that the Chinese view may eventually change.

Another ethical issue facing China is the black-market organ trade. Li cites the story of a teenage boy who sold one of his kidneys for approximately $3,500. While the boy sold his kidney voluntarily to have money to buy a new computer, other stories have involved coercion. In an article for the medical journal *The Lancet*, Ted Alcorn observes: "The scarcity of organs in China has also fostered a black market for illegal transplants, glimpsed by the public only through occasional reports such as the March, 2011, investigation by the Chinese newspaper *Southern Weekend*, which chronicled the story of a migrant worker named Hu Jie who was forced by traffickers to sell his kidney." The Chinese government has increased its efforts to fight illegal organ trafficking, including charging people with homicide if they compel another person to donate an organ. It is also considering financial incentives as a way to spur legal organ donation, which could reduce the appeal of a black market.

China is not alone in struggling to find the balance between increasing the availability of organs and ensuring its citizens donate organs in an ethical fashion. The authors in the following chapter debate the ethical challenges surrounding organ donation.

"A diagnosis of death by neurological criteria is theory, not scientific fact."

Organ Donation: The Inconvenient Truth

John B. Shea

In the following viewpoint, John B. Shea contends that the brain death and cardiac death criteria for organ donation are immoral. According to Shea, the Catholic Church permits organ donation from a deceased donor as long as the person is "certainly dead." However, he argues that there is scientific and medical evidence that people who are brain dead still have parts of their brain that are active, and some patients who have suffered cardiac death could still be revived. Shea is a physician who has written about bioethics for Catholic Insight.

As you read, consider the following questions:

1. As quoted by Shea, what does Alan Shewmon say is the result of brain death?
2. Which brain functions are ignored when a patient is declared brain dead, according to the author?
3. According to Shea, why are organ donors sometimes anesthetized?

Ever since organ donation after a declaration of "cardiac death" was first practised in the Ottawa Hospital in June 2006, Canadians have been subjected to an incessant drumbeat of rhetorical manipulation in the media in favour of organ donation. The following commentary is offered in order to inform the public about the truth in regard to both the moral principles and scientific facts pertaining to both the donation and harvesting of human organs for transplantation purposes. Many physicians have serious and well-considered concerns about the morality of human organ transplantation and about the fact that the general public has not been properly informed about what really happens when organs are retrieved.

Editor: *In July 2007, Britain's Chief Medical Officer repeated an earlier proposal to make a patient's consent for donating organs a* presumed *consent, in order to overcome a backlog of requests for organs. All patients, therefore, are counted as organ donors unless they specifically opt out. In Ontario, three legislators recently introduced private member's bills with similar provisions. Under this regime, organ donations become mandatory—an extremely dangerous development. The following essay explains why.*

Pope John Paul II, addressing the 18th International Congress of the Transplantation Society on August 29, 2000, stated that, "*Vital organs which occur singly* in the body can be removed only after death; that is, from the body of someone who is certainly dead . . . the death of a person is a single event consisting in the total disintegration of that unity and integrated whole that is the personal self. . . . The death of a person is an event which *no scientific technique or empirical method can identify directly*. . . . The "criteria" for ascertaining death used by medicine today should not be understood as the technical scientific determination of that *exact moment* of a person's death, but as a scientifically secure means of *identifying the biological signs that a person has died*." He further stated that "the criterion adopted in more recent times for ascertaining the fact of death—namely the *complete* and *irreversible* cessation of all brain activity—if rigorously applied, does not seem to conflict with the essential elements of a sound anthropology."[1] This was only a superficially apparent endorsement.

Alan Shewmon, vice-chair of neurology at the University of California, has stated that any attempt to define the unity of the "organism as a whole" versus multiplicity, a collection of organs and tissues, is, in theory, translatable from the philosophical to the physical domain. But he suspects that any attempt to operationally define "organism as a whole" with the goal of enabling unequivocal, non-arbitrary, dichotomous, categorization of all cases, is an exercise in futility. Shewmon also states "healthy living organisms are obviously integrated unities, that decomposing corpses are obviously not unities, and that there is a fuzzy area in between that is intrinsically undecidable."[2]

Church Re-Opens Debate

The arguments of some that complete cessation of brain activity was not equivalent to death was apparently enough to persuade Pope John Paul II to re-open the debate five years later. Just months before his death in April, 2005, he asked the Pontifical Academy for the Sciences to restudy the signs of death and get scientific verification that those signs were still valid.

Also, Pope Benedict XVI has asked that this debate be revived. On September 14, 2006, Bishop Sanchez, chancellor of the Academy, stated that the Academy had reaffirmed that brain death was equivalent to the death of a person. The debate is not over, however: Dr. Alan Shewmon, a participant in the Vatican study in 2006, has stated that brain death alone "results in a terminally ill patient, deeply comatose, but not a dead person." Bishop Sanchez said that he will have "to wait and see from the Vatican."

In his message on the World Day of the Sick, February 4, 2003, Pope John Paul II said, "It is never licit to kill one human being in order to save another." *The Catechism of the Catholic Church* states (paragraph 2296): "It is morally inadmissible directly to bring about the disabling mutilation or death of a human being, even in order to delay the death of other persons.[3]

Methods of Organ Retrieval

Today, organs are retrieved under four different sets of circumstances.

- From a living donor; for example, a single kidney or part of a liver. This presents no moral problem, provided there is properly informed consent and there is no major risk to the life or health of the donor

- From a person who is declared dead using the older criteria of loss of respiration and cardiac function along with *rigor mortis*. Tissues such as bone marrow, corneas, heart valves and skin may be removed. This procedure is morally acceptable

- After the patient has been declared "brain dead"

- After the patient has been declared to have suffered "cardiac death." The moral status of both "brain death" and "cardiac death" is questionable

Theory and Practice

Organs are obtained from an unconscious patient after he or she has been called "brain dead" using clinical and technologically acquired information, regarded as diagnostic. The public in general is not aware of the following serious criticisms of this kind of organ harvesting. The theory of brain death is highly controversial and can be used for utilitarian purposes.[4] The Pontifical Academy of Sciences declared brain death to be "the true criterion for death" in 1985 and again in 1989. However, in February of 2005, Pope John Paul II called for more precise means of establishing that the donor is dead before vital organs are removed. Organ transplants, he continued, are acceptable only when they are conducted in a manner "so as to guarantee respect for life and for the human person."[5]

The concept that whole brain death (irreversible loss of function of the cerebrum, cerebellum and brain stem) means the loss of integrated organic unity in a human being has been subjected to a powerful critique by neurologist Alan Shewmon.[6] Some physicians question whether we can be sure the entire brain is really dead in patients declared dead in the U.S. by "whole brain," or in the U.K. by "brain stem," criteria.[7] Neurological criteria are not sufficient for declaration of death when an intact cardio-respiratory system is functioning. These criteria test for the absence of some specific brain reflexes. Functions of the brain that are not considered are temperature control, blood pressure, cardiac rate and salt and water balance. When a patient is declared brain dead, these functions are not only still present, but also frequently active.

There is no consensus on diagnostic criteria for brain death. They are the subject of intense international debate. Various sets of neurological criteria for the diagnosis of brain death are used. A person could be diagnosed as brain dead if one set is used and not be diagnosed as brain dead if another is used.[8,9,10,11]

A diagnosis of death by neurological criteria is theory, not scientific fact. Also, irreversibility of neurological function is a prognosis, not a medically observable fact. There is also evidence of poor compliance with accepted guidelines of brain death.[12]

Utilitarian Rationale

Brain death can be used for purely utilitarian purposes. In 2005, Dr. Robert Spaemann, a former philosopher at the University of Munich, told the Pontifical Academy of Sciences that the brain death approach to defining death reflects a new set of priorities. It was no longer the interest of the dying to avoid being declared "dead" prematurely, but the community's interest in declaring a dying person dead as soon as possible.

Two reasons are given: 1) guaranteeing legal immunity for discontinuing life-prolonging measures that would constitute a financial and personal burden for family members and society alike, and 2) collecting vital organs for the purpose of saving the lives of other human beings by transplantation.[13]

The goal is to move to a society where people see organ donation as a social responsibility and where donating organs would be accepted as a normal part of dying. In cases where a person chose to withhold recording a specific choice about donating his or her organs, the surviving family members would agree to donation.[14] In the U.S., federal regulations require institutions to contact local organ procurement organizations concerning death, or impending death, to insure that the family will be approached at the appropriate time by a professional skilled in presenting the proposal of organ donation.

Vatican Debate

Bishop Fabian Bruskewitz of Lincoln, Nebraska told the Pontifical Academy at its 2005 meeting that "no respectable, learned and accepted moral Catholic theologian has said that the words of Jesus regarding laying down one's life for one's friends (John 15:13) is a command or even a licence for suicidal consent for the benefit of another's continuation of earthly life." The bishop then observed that current technology enables doctors to monitor brain activity "in the outer one or two centimetres of the brain." He asked, "Do we have, then, moral certitude in any way that can be called apodictic, regarding even the existence, much less the cessation, of brain activity?"[15]

In 2006, the Pontifical Academy published a statement titled, "Why the concept of brain death is valid as a definition of death." Breaking protocol, several participants in a 2005 Vatican-sponsored conference on the ethics of declaring someone brain dead have published the papers they delivered at the debate. The publication of those papers, which the Vatican had decided not to publish, is evidence of strong feelings about brain death by a minority of members of the Pontifical Academy for Life. Roberto De Mattei, vice-president of the National Research

There Is No Consensus on Brain Death

One can be declared "brain dead" by one set of criteria, but alive by another or perhaps all others; in other words, one could be declared dead in one state and alive in another. This quandary has persisted to the present. In the January 2008 edition of *Neurology*, it was reported that there is no consensus about which of the hundreds of disparate sets of criteria should be used to declare a person "brain dead." The pro-life author warned that Western society is reaching a point, if it is not already there, where the moment of death will be determined not by objective bodily changes but rather the philosophy of personhood by those in power.

American Catholic, *"What Happened to the Hippocratic Oath?," May 5, 2010.*

Council of Italy, told *Catholic News Service* on April 20, 2007 that, "The concern of many is that the Vatican has not taken the appropriate position when doubts exist about the end of human life. . . . The moment of separation of the soul from the body is shrouded in mystery, just as the moment when a soul enters a person is."[15]

Harvard's Oxymoron

The 1968 Harvard Ad Hoc Committee for Irreversible Coma published criteria that held that any organ that no longer functions, or has the possibility of functioning again, is, for all practical purposes, *if not in reality,* dead. They then described the criteria for the diagnosis of irreversible coma and its concomitantly permanent non-functioning brain. They equated the state of coma with brain death and then declared the patient brain-dead. They implied that brain death should be regarded as death, because it inevitably leads to death and that the person in irreversible coma is, for all practical purposes, *if not in reality*, dead. Untold semantic confusion has followed this oxymoronic notion.[16]

The Deadly Apnea Test

Every set of criteria for "brain death" includes an apnea test, considered the most important step in the diagnosis of brain death. The ventilator is discontinued. "Apnea" is the absence of breathing. The only purpose of this test is to determine if the patient is unable to breathe on his or her own, in order to declare "brain death." It aggravates the patient's condition and is commonly done without the knowledge or consent of family members. The ventilator is turned off for up to 10 minutes, carbon dioxide increases in the blood and the blood pressure may drop, indicating that cardiac arrest has occurred. The test significantly impairs the possibility of recovery and can lead to the death of the patient through a heart attack or irreversible brain damage. Dr. Yoshio Watenabe, a cardiologist from Natoya, Japan, stated that if patients were not subjected to the apnea test, they could have a 60 per cent chance of recovery to normal life if treated with timely therapeutic hypothermia (cooling). Note the similarity to cardiac death, later described.[17]

Some form of anesthesia is needed to prevent the donor from moving during removal of the organs. The donor's blood pressure may rise during surgical removal. Similar changes take place during ordinary surgical procedures only if the depth of anesthesia is inadequate. Body movement and a rise in blood pressure are due to the skin incision and surgical procedure if the donor is not anesthetized. Is it not reasonable to consider that the donor may feel pain? In some cases, drugs to paralyze muscle contraction are given to prevent the donor from moving during removal of the organs. Yet, sometimes no anesthesia is administered to the donor. Movement by the donor is distressing to doctors and nurses. Perhaps this is another reason why anesthesia and drugs to paralyze the muscles are usually given.

Organ Harvesting After "Cardiac Death"

Brain death has been used as a means for the moral validation of the retrieval of human organs for transplant since the late 1960s, and "brain dead" patients have been the main source of organs over the years ever since. However, demand for organs has increasingly exceeded supply. In 1993, a new way for categorizing patients as "dead" was conceived. According to a protocol developed at the University of Pittsburgh, a patient could be declared dead, even though not "brain dead," if he or she was declared to have suffered "irreversible loss of circulatory and respiratory function." The Institute of Medicine found that in so-called "controlled non-heartbeating donation," a typical patient would be five to 55 years old, would have suffered a severe head injury, would not be brain dead, would not be a drug user or HIV-positive and would be free from cancer or sepsis. This patient would frequently be unconscious as a result of a car crash.

Typically, the patient would be in an emergency department, in coma, and on a ventilator. If the physician decided that treatment was futile, he asked the relatives' permission to withdraw ventilation and then for their permission to remove organs, if the patient's heart had stopped beating. Ventilation was then withdrawn. If the heart stopped beating within an hour, the surgeon waited two to five minutes before taking out the organs. If the heart had not stopped beating within an hour, the patient would be returned to a hospital bed to die without any further treatment. Note that the patient's physician has a conflict of interest. The longer he waits, the less suitable the organs are for transplant due to damage from lack of oxygenation. The sooner the doctor declares treatment futile, the less chance the patient has of spontaneous recovery.[18]

These procedures are performed despite animal studies and clinical experience that shows even complete recovery of consciousness is possible several minutes after the heart stops, if resuscitative efforts succeed. This kind of resuscitation has been reported after more than 10 minutes of cardiac electric asystole in humans.[19] The fact that the heart stops beating due to ventricular fibrillation, as occurs in a heart attack, does not indicate irreversible cessation of cardiac activity.[20] The application of criteria for organ donation after cardiac death becomes questionable since artificial circulatory and ventilatory support is sometimes resumed after death in order to maintain the viability of abdominal and thoracic organs in potential donors.[21] Extracorporeal circulatory support can lead to return of neurological function in people who were neurologically intact before cardiac death.[22,23]

Finally, it is now widely known that a patient whose heart has stopped beating for 15 minutes after a heart attack can recover if he is treated by cooling the body to 33°C, cardio-pulmonary bypass, cardioplegia (stopping the heart beat chemically) and a slow increase in oxygenation for 24 hours. Up to 80 per cent of these patients can be discharged from hospital, 55 per cent having a good neurological outcome. Clearly, the assumption made by physicians that a patient is dead five minutes after the heart has stopped beating is incorrect.[24]

An ominous and disturbing development is a recent widespread move to involve *palliative caregivers* in the organ donation process. Those care givers are said to provide "skills and principles applicable to donation after cardiac death." In effect, they are to be the agents of a soft-sell program to make the family "feel comfortable and supported during this extremely difficult time." This movement is in keeping with the Institute of Medicine Report Brief, 2006, on "Organ Donation: Opportunities for Action." The IOM goal is "to move toward a society where people see organ donation as a social responsibility" and where "donating organs would be accepted as a normal part of dying and, in cases where a patient died without recording a specific choice about donation of his or her organs, the surviving family members would be comfortable giving permission."[25]

Comment: *Organ donation can be a moral good if the means used to obtain the organs is itself morally good. The circumstances under which this holds true have been described. The critical question is whether a person is truly dead when declared "brain dead" or to have suffered "cardiac death." The answer, in light of the scientific evidence, is that it has not been established cardiac or brain death criteria indicate the real death of a patient with certainty. Mauro Cozzoli, writing about the status of the embryo, has stated, "The uncertainty with regard to whether we are dealing with a human individual is not an abstract doubt, regarding a theory, principle, or doctrinal position* (dubium uris). *As such, it is a doubt about a fact concerning the life of a human being, his existence here and now* (dubium facti). *As such, "it creates the same obligations as certainty."[26]*

The object of the will is determined by both the agent's motive (finis operantis) *and by the physical character, the integral nature of the external act* (finis operis). *The physical and clinical realities of an action, whether actual or potential, must not be ignored or denied.[27] Those caregivers in Catholic hospitals who administer levonorgestrel, an abortifacient, to a woman who has been raped, ignore or deny the fact that it is impossible to exclude the possibility that she has ovulated and may be pregnant. Those who harvest organs after brain death or cardiac death similarly ignore or deny the possibility that the "donor" may be alive. Professor Joseph Seifert, from the International Academy of Philosophy in Lichtenstein, states that medical ethicists should invoke the traditional moral teaching of the Catholic Church that "even if a small, reasonable doubt exists that our acts kill a living human person, we must abstain from them."[28]*

The declaration of brain death or cardiac death is not sufficient to arrive at moral certitude. The recovery of organs based on that declaration is, therefore, immoral.

References

1. Address of the Holy Father, John Paul II, to the 18th International Congress of the Transplantation Society. August 29, 2000.
2. Dr. Alan Shewmon and Elizabeth Seitz Shewmon. "The Semiotics of Death and Its Medical Implications," *Brain Death and Disorders of Consciousness*. Edited by Machado and Shewmon. Kluwer Academic/Plenum publishers, New York, 2004, pp. 105–6.
3. Carol Glatz. "Vatican resuscitates issue of whether brain death means total death." Vatican Letter, Catholic New Service. Sept. 15, 2006, backgrounder xxxi.
4. Capron, A.M. "Brain Death—Well Settled, Yet Still Unresolved." *New England Journal of Medicine*. April 19, 2001, vol. 344 (16).
5. Pope John Paul II. Letter to the Pontifical Academy of Sciences. Feb. 3, 2005.
6. D. Alan Shewmon. "Recovery from Brain Death. A Neurologist's Apologia." *Linacre Quarterly*, Feb. 1997, 30–96.
7. Donald W. Evans, retired physician, Queen's College, Cambridge. *Journal of Medical Ethics*. April 11, 2007.
8. Wijdicks, E.F. *Neurology*. 2002, Jan. 8; 58(1): 20–25.
9. Haupt, W.F., Rudolf J. "European brain death codes: a comparison of national guidelines." *J. Neurol*. 1999, June; 246(6): 432–7.
10. Evans, D.W. and Potts, M. Brain death. *BMJ*, 2002; 325:598.
11. David W. Evans. Open letter to Prof. E. F. M. Wijdics. Dec. 11, 2001, www.bmj.com.
12. Wang M.Y. et al. Neurosurgery. 2002, Sept; 51(3): 751–5.
13. Institute of Medicine, National Academy of Sciences, Report Brief, Organ Donation: Opportunities for Action, Committee on Increasing Role of Organ Donation. May, 2006.
14. D. Truog et al. Recommendations for End-of-Life Care in the Intensive Care Unit. The Ethics Committee of the Society of Critical Care. *Crit. Care Med*. 2001, vol. 29, no. 12, pp. 2332–2334.
15. Paul A. Byrne *et al*. "Brain Death is Not Death!" Source: Essay—Meeting of the Political Academy of Sciences, in early February, Paul Byrne to the *Compassionate Health Care Network*. March 29, 2005, via email.
16. See reference 6.
17. Ari R. Joffe, critical care physician, Stollery Children's Hospital, University of Alberta, e-letter to J.R. Cuo *et al*. Time dependent validity in the diagnosis of brain death using transcranial Doppler. *J. Neurol Neurosurg Psychiatry*. 2006; 77: 646–649.
18. Institute of Medicine. "Non-Heart-Beating Organ Transplantation—Medical and Ethical Issues of Procurement." 1997, National Academy Press, Washington, D.C.
19. Adhiyaman V., Sundaram R. The Lazarus phenomenon. *J. R. Coll. Physicians Edinb.* 2002, 32: 9–13.
20. American Heart Association. Management of Cardiac Arrest. *Circulation*. 2005; 112:IV 58-IV66.
21. Institute of Medicine Committee on Non-Heart-Beating Transplantation. *The scientific and ethical basis for practice and protocols, executive summary*. Washington, (D.C.): National Academy Press, 2000.
22. Magliocca, J. F. et al. Extracorporeal support for organ donation after cardiac death effectively expands the donor pool. *J Trauma*. 2005; 58:1095–1201.
23. Younger, J.G. et al. Extracorporeal resuscitation of cardiac arrest. *Acad Emerg Med.* 1999: 6: 700–7.
24. Weisfeldt, M.L., Becker L. "Resuscitation After Cardiac Arrest" A 3-phase Time-Sensitive Model. *JAMA*. Dec. 18, 2002, vol. 288, no. 23, pp. 3035–8.

25. Catherine McVearry Kelso, MD. et al. Palliative Care Consultation in the Process of Organ Donation after Cardiac Death. *Journal of Palliative Medicine*, vol. 10, no. 11, 2007.

26. Prof. Mauro Cozzoli, The Human Embryo: Ethical and Normative Aspects. The Identity and Status of the Human Embryo. Proceedings of the Third Assembly of the Pontifical Academy for Life, Vatican City. Feb. 14–16, 1997, p. 271, *Libreria Editrice Vaticana*, 00120. Citta Dei of Vaticano.

27. Steven Long, Regarding the Nature of the Object of the Moral Act According to St. Thomas Aquinas. The Thomistic Institute, 2001, maritain.nd.edu/jiuc/ti01/long.htm.

28. See reference 15.

Addendum

The case for considering "brain death" as equivalent to true death has undergone further trenchant scientific and philosophical critique.[1,2,3]

The notion of irreversible loss of circulatory and respiratory function as a criterion for determining death has also been seriously challenged. This notion means either that the heart cannot be restarted spontaneously (a weaker definition) or that the heart cannot be started despite standard cardio-pulmonary resuscitation (a stronger definition.) The stronger definition of irreversibility as meaning "can never be done" implies that *at no time* can organ procurement be permissible, because future possibilities of resuscitation can never be ruled out. The weaker definition, in practice, considers the patient dead based on the patient's moral choice to forego resuscitative interventions. The problem is that, first, the issue is not whether to resuscitate a person, but is the person truly dead? And secondly, that resuscitative interventions *are performed* during the procurement process to keep organs viable for transplantation after cessation of vital functions; for example, the use of cardio bypass machines, etc. This can result in a return of heart and brain function and even a return to consciousness.[4]

The application of criteria for irreversible cessation of neurologic, circulatory and respiratory functions requires a waiting time well in excess of 10 minutes to give more precision to the determination of death or organ procurement.[5,6,7,8,9,10]

References

1. Potts M., Byrne P.A., Nilges R.G. *Beyond brain death: the case against brain based criteria for human death.* Dordecht: Kluwer Academic Publishers, 2000.
2. Shewmon, D.A. "Brain body disconnection: implications for the theoretical basis of 'brain death'" in De Mattia R., *Finis Vitae—is brain death still life?* 211-50. Roma: Consiglio Nazionale della Richerche, 2006.
3. Truog, R.D., "Brain death—too flawed to endure, too ingrained to abandon." *J Law Med. Eth.* 2007: 35(2): 273–81.
4. Verheijde J.L., Rady, M.Y., McGregor, J. "Recovery of transplantable organs after cardiac or circulatory death: transforming the paradigm of the ethics of organ donation." *Philosophy, Ethics and Humanities in Medicine.* 2007, 2:8, http://www.peh.med.com /content/2/1/8.
5. Kootstra, G. The asystolic or non-heart beating donor. *Transplantation.* 1997, 63(7): 917–21.
6. Weber, M. et al. Kidney Transplantation from Donors Without a Heartbeat. N Eng J Med. 2002, 347 (4): 248–255.
7. Daar, A. S: Non-heartbeating donation: 10 evidence-based ethical recommendations. *Transplant Proceed.* 2004, 26: 1885–1887.
8. Wijdics, E.F., Diringer, M.N. Electro-cardiographic activity after terminal cardiac arrest in neurocatastrophies. *Neurology.* 2004, 62(4): 673–674.
9. Bos, M.A. Ethical and legal issues in non-heartbeating organ donation. *Transplantation.* 2005, 79(9): 1143–1147.
10. Bell, M., MD. Non-heartbeating organ donation: clinical process and fundamental issues. *Br J Anaesth.* 2005, 94(4): 474–478.

*"Brain death criteria are used legally in
all 50 states to pronounce patients dead."*

Recovery of Organs Based on Brain Death Is Ethical

James M. DuBois

*Brain death is an ethical way to determine that a patient is eligible
to become an organ donor, James M. DuBois argues in the following viewpoint. He maintains that while the general public does not
understand facts about brain death, Catholic pro-life groups' objections are based on incorrect assumptions about what it means to
be human. DuBois concludes that rejecting organ donation based
on this criticism would negatively impact those most in need. Du-
Bois is the department chair of health-care ethics at Saint Louis
University.*

As you read, consider the following questions:

1. As quoted by DuBois, what does the Catechism of the
   Catholic Church say about organ donation?
2. What is the difference between brain-dead patients and
   patients in permanent vegetative states, as explained by
   the author?

3. In DuBois's view, how do some opponents to brain-death criteria misunderstand human biology?

Few medical procedures have proven to be as effective in saving lives as organ transplantation. Patients on the verge of death from organ failure often live a decade or longer after receiving a transplant. The Catholic Church, and the late Pope John Paul II in particular, have been enthusiastic proponents of this extraordinary medical procedure. According to the *Catechism of the Catholic Church*, "organ donation after death is a noble and meritorious act and is to be encouraged as an expression of generous solidarity." Yet despite the church's longstanding support for organ donation, some Catholic pro-life groups challenge practices essential to it.

Challenging the Brain-Death Criteria

The latest challenge pertains to so-called brain-death criteria, which are used to declare death in over 90 percent of all cases of organ donation in the United States. In a front-page article in *L'Osservatore Romano*, Lucetta Scaraffia, a professor of history at La Sapienza University in Rome and a frequent contributor to the Vatican newspaper, argued that the Catholic Church must revisit the question of brain death because it rests on an understanding of human life that is contrary to Catholic teaching. While Federico Lombardi, S.J., director of the Vatican press office, quickly stated that Scaraffia spoke for herself and not for the magisterium, her article shows there is disagreement within the church on the question of organ donation.

Earlier this year [2009], Paul Byrne, M.D., a former president of the Catholic Medical Association and a long-time opponent of brain-death criteria, published a letter on the Web site Renew America arguing that God's law and the natural law preclude "the transplantation of unpaired vital organs, an act which causes the death of the 'donor' and violates the fifth commandment of the divine Decalogue, 'Thou shalt not kill' [Deuteronomy]." The letter was signed by over 400 individuals, including at least three Catholic bishops and many pro-life program directors.

In 1985 and 1989 the Pontifical Academy of Science studied the question of brain death and concluded that neurological criteria are the most appropriate criteria for determining the death of a human being. In the academy's view, one really should not speak of "brain death"—as if only the brain had died—but rather of the death of the human being, which may be determined neurologically.

In 2000 Pope John Paul II expressed support for organ donation and the use of neurological criteria. He wrote: "The criterion adopted in more recent times for ascertaining the fact of death, namely the complete and irreversible cessation of all brain activity, if rigorously applied, does not seem to conflict with the essential elements of a sound anthropology." He concluded that "a health worker professionally responsible for ascertaining death can use these criteria. . . ." Moreover, he strongly reasserted his support for organ donation, calling it a "genuine act of love" and noting that he had earlier called it a "way of nurturing a genuine culture of life."

To be fair, the Pontifical Academy of Science has no moral teaching authority, and a papal allocution is not the same as a papal encyclical or conciliar teaching. Still, it is ironic that many of the same people who continue to question brain-death criteria after John Paul II's allocution argue that the same pope's allocution on artificial nutrition and hydration for patients in a permanent vegetative state has decisively settled that matter.

Addressing the Objections to Brain-Death Criteria

For many people, concerns about brain death arise from a simple misunderstanding of the facts. I have spent years studying how the general public and health professionals understand death and organ donation. People in focus groups and surveys often confuse brain death with P.V.S. [persistent vegetative state]. Yet

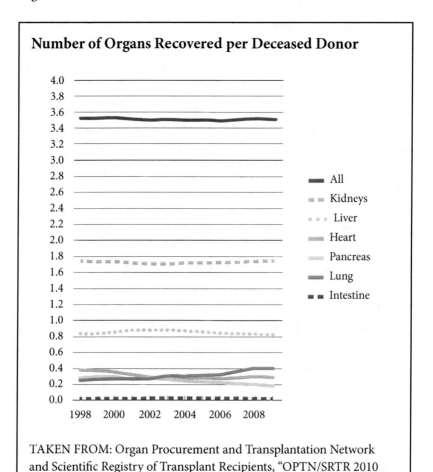

Number of Organs Recovered per Deceased Donor

Legend:
- All
- Kidneys
- Liver
- Heart
- Pancreas
- Lung
- Intestine

TAKEN FROM: Organ Procurement and Transplantation Network and Scientific Registry of Transplant Recipients, "OPTN/SRTR 2010 Annual Report: Deceased Organ Donation," 2010.

P.V.S. patients breathe spontaneously and have sleep-wake cycles. Brain-dead bodies depend upon artificial ventilation; without it there would be no respiration and no heartbeat. Moreover, many think it is possible to recover from brain death, just as patients sometimes recover from deep coma. Yet there is no documented case of a patient recovering from brain death, despite some popular reports of misdiagnosed brain death. An organ that has been deprived of oxygen sufficiently long will die, and it is medically impossible to change dead brain cells to living brain cells. Finally, about half of Americans do not know that brain death criteria are used legally in all 50 states to pronounce patients dead. They are also used in nearly all Catholic hospitals in the United States.

While these factual misunderstandings are common among the general public, they are not the source of the concerns expressed by Catholic pro-life groups. Their objections to brain-death criteria tend to be more philosophical. In a recent article in *The National Catholic Bioethics Quarterly*, I have tried to address some of these concerns. Here I will summarize three key points.

Human development. Lucetta Scaraffia and others have voiced concern that if we decide a human being is dead because he or she lacks a functioning brain, then we will deny that embryos are human until they form a brain. However, we are developmental creatures: in our earliest days of development in the uterus, we do not depend upon a brain to live. Yet as we grow, we come to depend upon a functioning brain; and when it dies, we die. To argue that support for brain death criteria calls into question the status of early human life is to misunderstand basic human biology.

The unity of the human being. According to some Catholic pro-life advocates, the brain death criteria accepted by the larger medical community rest on a "dualistic" view of the human being that assumes the human soul is radically distinct from the human body. They argue that if the soul is the life principle of the body and if an artificially maintained brain-dead body shows some signs of life, like a beating heart, then the soul must be present. Like many members of the Catholic medical community, I do not dispute the Catholic understanding of life and death; we take seriously the fact that the soul and its proper functions are intimately bound with the body. Yet a mature human body that is functionally decapitated is no longer a living human being.

Ken Iserson, M.D., a professor of emergency medicine at the University of Arizona, cites the Talmud when describing brain death: "The death throes of a decapitated man are not signs of life any more than is the twitching of a lizard's amputated tail." If one rejects the notion that a decapitated body is a dead body, then one is left with a conclusion repugnant to common sense and good metaphysics: a severed head and a decapitated body would both have to be considered living human beings if separately maintained alive (a view held by at least one opponent of brain death criteria). In fact, to be wholly consistent, one would need to hold that each is independently the same living human being that existed prior to the decapitation—a view that flatly contradicts the unity required to be human.

Strange case reports. Following brain death, most bodies spontaneously lose circulation within days, even when they are artificially ventilated and provided with aggressive critical care. But there have been exceptional case reports of prolonged "survival" of the ventilated body. These are not misdiagnoses. In some cases, the entire brain liquefies and extremities begin to turn black. Despite continued circulation, there is no room for speculation that such bodies are any more conscious than a corpse that has been buried, and the likelihood of recovery is the same. Professor Scaraffia has noted that there have also been cases of pregnant women who were pronounced brain dead; yet with artificial ventilation and aggressive support their bodies sustained pregnancies until viability. But the fact that many parts of the body may survive and function for a time is wholly compatible with death of the human being. This is precisely what makes organ transplantation possible. The human heart may beat outside of the human body in a bucket of ice, and may even be transplanted and made to function again inside another human being. That the placenta and womb may survive and function in a body maintained artificially is similarly amazing, but it does not indicate that the womb belongs to a living human being. Importantly, none of these cases present "new data" that became available only after John Paul II's allocution, and thus they do not merit a re-examination of church teaching. They are well known, even if strange and rare, phenomena.

Treating Donors with Respect

In the end, I think these philosophical disputes about brain death are actually motivated by a much deeper, more fundamental opposition to organ donation. This is illustrated by the resistance pro-life groups have offered to other kinds of organ donation, including donation after cardiac death. This opposition ultimately is driven by two deeper concerns that often go unarticulated.

First, organ donation risks treating human beings or their deceased bodies as "objects." In John Paul II's 2000 allocution on organ donation and brain death, he stated that "any procedure which tends to commercialize human organs or to consider them as items of exchange or trade must be considered morally unacceptable, because to use the body as an 'object' is to violate the dignity of the human person." He also noted that organ donation requires the informed consent of the patient or the patient's family. Yet the continual shortage of organs leads some policymakers to consider payments for organs and even organ procurement without expressed consent. Overly hasty pronouncements of brain death—which are rare but have received considerable attention in recent years—also reinforce suspicions that a concern for organ donation is trumping care for patients.

The ethical question at hand is how we should deal with the risk of treating persons as objects or commodities. It is worth recalling that Hans Jonas, one of the more famous opponents of brain-death criteria, also expressed deep reservations about medical research in general, which has yielded numerous treatments, vaccines and cures. Jonas feared that such research tends by its very nature to treat human subjects as "objects" or things. But the Catholic Church does not view medical research as intrinsically wrong for that reason; rather, it suggests how research may be conducted respectfully. It is the same with organ donation.

A second obstacle to organ donation within some Catholic circles rests on a misunderstanding of the so-called precautionary principle. This principle has been used in Catholic social teaching and basically urges caution in the face of uncertainty regarding grave risks of harm (for example, the possible harm from genetic modification). Paul Byrne, M.D., and colleagues seem to seek an absolute certainty that death has occurred, one marked by the destruction of all major organ systems. This is why Dr. Byrne opposes not only brain death, but also deceased-organ donation; by the time he would consider a body dead, no organs would be healthy enough to transplant. Yet this desire for absolute certainty conflicts with what Pope John Paul II wrote on the subject. He stated that "a health worker professionally responsible for ascertaining death can use these [neurological] criteria in each individual case as the basis for arriving at that degree of assurance in ethical judgment which moral teaching describes as 'moral certainty.'" He added that this "moral certainty is considered the necessary and sufficient basis for an ethically correct course of action."

Determining death in the context of organ donation is challenging and will likely remain controversial for the simple reason that death must be determined quickly lest all transplantable organs die with the human being. Nevertheless, the decision to reject organ donation in the name of precaution is not without cost. Patients in need of an organ transplant will die years earlier than necessary, and families who often find organ donation consoling will be bereft of the opportunity to find some meaning in their loss. We may not do evil that good may come of it, but neither should we bury our talents out of fear.

| "Through organ donation, prisoners can preserve a sense of self worth and dignity."

Organ Donation by a Prisoner: Legal and Ethical Considerations

Stuart J. Bagatell, Donald P. Owens, and Marc J. Kahn

In the following viewpoint, Stuart J. Bagatell, Donald P. Owens, and Marc J. Kahn recount an experience serving on an ethics committee where they allowed a prisoner to donate a kidney. According to the authors, the donor in this particular case was compensated fairly, without it being a prohibited sale. In addition, they argue that the donor was not coerced into making the decision and was undergoing a low-risk operation. The authors conclude that prisoners have the autonomy to make the decision to donate organs. Bagatell is on the staff at JFK Medical Center in Atlantis, Florida; Owens is an associate professor of medicine and psychiatry at Tulane University's school of medicine; and Kahn is a professor of medicine and a senior associate dean at the Tulane School of Medicine.

As you read, consider the following questions:

1. What is "compensation," as defined by the authors?
2. In the case described by the authors, why did coercion not play a role?
3. What is the mortality rate for kidney donation, according to the authors?

It is axiomatic that the act of surgery is legal assault unless the consent of the patient or his legal representative is obtained. Consent has been defined as informed consent obtained without duress. How voluntary a contribution does a brother make when he is informed that unless he offers his kidney, his twin brother will die? Can there be greater coercion that the sanction of family and friends in such a situation where the probability of successful transplantation is indeed very good? Yet what value judgment would society place in the rich industrialist who buys a kidney for his dying son for $100,000 from a poor employee in one of his factories? What about prisoners who volunteer?[1]

Rabbi Tendler

Being a member of an ethics committee is something which most physicians probably have not experienced. Academic physicians are frequently called upon to serve on committees in addition to taking care of patients and teaching. However, as most physicians are not theologians or moralists, ethics committees strive to include individuals with varied backgrounds including members of the clergy, nurses, psychologists, psychiatrists, oncologists, neonatologists, lawyers, business administrators, and students. With a collective intelligence, common sense, and experience, the goal of an ethics committee is to come to the "right" conclusion, similar to deliberations of a jury. This is often difficult when the motives of the patients involved are in question.

The Case

The Tulane abdominal transplant team had identified a potential kidney donor. This potential donor, however, had been arrested in Louisiana on charges of theft over $500. In addition, the potential donor had a warrant outstanding in Tennessee for probation violation after a conviction of theft over $1000. During the time between leaving Tennessee and his arrest in Louisiana, the potential donor befriended the potential recipient. The recipient allowed the potential donor to live in a house on his property, providing the potential donor with gainful employment and the chance for a brighter future. Over the course of a few months, the potential donor learned about the recipient's medical ailment, and for reasons unknown to the ethics committee, offered to donate a kidney to the recipient. To complicate matters further, the recipient made a promise to the potential donor that he would become the "godfather" of the donor's child following the transplant. Although the terms of this agreement were not specified, we assumed this meant that the recipient agreed to help care for and raise the potential donor's child which would likely involve some monetary assistance.

The charges in Louisiana were eventually dropped. The district attorney in Louisiana and the district attorney in Tennessee discussed the matter, and the potential donor was released from prison on his own recognizance with the understanding that once the potential donor was fit enough (assuming the kidney transplant went forward) to face the charges against him in Tennessee, the potential donor would be expected to appear in court. The question posed by the transplant team to the ethics committee was: "Would it be ethical to allow this particular living kidney donation to take place?"

Legal Implications

The first issue to address in the case presented is the legality of the proposed organ donation. In this regard, there are two main questions to consider: 1) Does the "deal" between the donor and recipient (exchange of "godfather" designation for kidney) constitute a sale of a human organ, rendering it illegal under current US law? Although the potential donor was no longer a prisoner, it was still interesting and relevant to answer. 2) Can a prisoner legally donate an organ?

As for the first question, the distinction between gift, sale, and compensation needs to be made. The definition of a *gift* is something voluntarily transferred by one person to another without compensation. In this case, the potential donor is not gifting his kidney as there is a quid pro quo, namely the promise of continued care for the potential donor's son in exchange for the organ. Therefore, a discussion concerning the ethics and legality of gift giving is not necessary in this case.

Unlike a gift, a sale refers to the transfer of ownership and title to property from one person to another for a price. Referring to the sale of organs for transplantation, Al Gore said, "It is against our system of values to buy and sell parts of human beings. It is wrong." In 1984, the same year Gore made his statement, the National Organ Transplant Act prohibited the sale of several organs and body parts for purposes of transplantation (42#U.S.C. 274 (1984)).[2,3] Therefore, according to US law, the idea of body parts being relegated to the status of "property" that can be sold for money is wrong. In other cultures, however, there are differences in ethical principles. For example, in Iran, there has been a program of compensated kidney donation from living unrelated donors since 1997. In that nation and culture, it is believed that depriving an organ donor of legitimate compensation is not ethically defensible.[4] Similarly, with respect to organ transplantation, Pope Pius XII declared in 1956 that "It would be going too far to declare immoral every acceptance or demand of payment. It is not necessarily a fault to accept it."[5] In this case, there is no evidence of a sale taking place.

Compensation is defined as something that constitutes an equivalent exchange of one thing for another. Compensation does not necessarily imply a direct exchange of money for goods and services. Recognizing the need for transplantable organs, in 2002 the United States considered compensation by way of a tax incentive for organ donation when two bills proposed within the House of Representatives called for an amendment to the IRS Code. The Gift of Life Tax Credit (GOLTC) Act and the Help Organ Procurement Expand (HOPE) Act both presented a refundable credit to individuals or to the estates of those who agree either to be living donors or to donate their organs upon death. The GOLTC act would have refunded $10,000 to the estates of individuals and the HOPE Act would have offered a refund of $2500 to qualified persons.[6] Although both bills died in committee, it seems that our government at least considered compensation for organ donation. This idea of a tax credit for organ donors appears to be more palatable than the direct selling of organs.

Returning to our case, a fair arrangement for compensation was agreed upon; the potential donor giving the potential recipient a new start to his life, and the recipient giving the donor's child a chance for a new start to his life. Section 274e(a) of the National Organ Transplant Act of 1984 states:

> It shall be unlawful for any person to knowingly acquire, receive, or otherwise transfer any human organ for valuable consideration for use in human transplantation if the transfer affects interstate commerce.

It is fair to say that caring for the donor's child would not affect interstate commerce. Thus, the recipient's agreement to care for the donor's child in exchange for receipt of the donor's kidney

Preliminary Results of a Survey of Death Row Inmates About Organ Donation

Surveys were mailed to all 37 inmates serving time on death row in Oregon as of September 2011. . . . 23/37 responded to the survey (62% response rate), 22/37 (or 59.5%) completed the survey in its entirety.

In your opinion, should inmates on death row be allowed to register as organ donors?
20/23 responded "yes" (86.9%)

Which of the following statements characterize your attitude toward organ donation by inmates on death row? (select all that apply)

Inmates on death row should not be allowed to register as organ donors
2/23 (8.7%) selected this response

Inmates on death row should not be encouraged to become organ donors
18/23 (78.2%) selected this response

Organ donation is one way death row inmates can help other people
19/23 (82.6%) selected this response

Inmates on death row should be allowed to become organ donors
17/23 (73.9%) selected this response

Inmates on death row should be allowed and encouraged to become organ donors
8/23 (34.8%) selected this response

Western Oregon University, "Organ Donation Survey Preliminary Findings," www.gavelife.org, 2012.

does not fall within the Act's definition of a prohibited sale of an organ.

The next issue to consider is the legality of a prisoner donating an organ. Both district attorneys involved with this case were in agreement about the release of the potential donor on his own recognizance. Therefore, the potential donor would no longer be a prisoner at the time of transplant. Regardless, Louisiana Revised Statute 15:831 regarding medical care of inmates expressly permits inmates to donate organs for transplant:

> No monies appropriated to the department from the state general fund or from dedicated funds shall be used for medical costs associated with organ transplants for inmates or for the purposes of providing cosmetic medical treatment of inmates, unless the condition necessitating such treatment or organ transplant arises or results from an accident or situation which was the fault of the department or resulted from an action or lack of action on the part of the department. However, nothing in this Section shall prohibit an inmate from donating his vital organs for transplant purposes.

Ethical Considerations

A recent consensus on live organ donation states, that "a person who gives consent to be a live organ donor should be competent, willing to donate, free from coercion, medically and psychosocially suitable, fully informed of the risks and benefits as a donor, and fully informed of the risks, benefits and alternative treatment available to the recipient."[7] Therefore, in order to properly respond to the request from the transplant team, we needed to account for each of these facets of the case.

Before any transplant at Tulane University Hospital, a psychologist performs a thorough evaluation of the donor and comments on whether or not he is suitable for transplant. The psychosocial evaluation of the potential donor includes, among other things, assessment for vulnerability to coercion and the nature of the relationship between the donor and the recipient. In this case, we received a report that affirmed the donor was in fact competent to make the decision to donate his kidney.

Another question that remained to be answered was whether or not the donor was free from coercion. Prisoners are in a very vulnerable position. The conditions of imprisonment are themselves coercive and not conducive to free decision making, but this should be seen as a vulnerability that should not disqualify a person from becoming an organ donor.[8] There is a fine line between coercion and the reciprocal nature of friendship. In this case, there was a question concerning the relationship between the potential donor and potential recipient making it unclear whether or not the donor was free from coercion. An argument could be made that the donor was being coerced by the recipient through the promise of the recipient serving as godfather to the donor's son. Friendships, however, are based on mutual respect, and reciprocal exchange of care and concern. In this case, the friendship was forged over a period of months when the recipient gave lodging and gainful employment to the potential donor. The result was the building of a trust between the two which resulted not only in the willingness to donate a kidney, but to the potential donor trusting the recipient to care for his son when he could not. As a result of this friendship, coercion did not appear to play a role.

Regarding the issue of safety of the procedure, the physicians on the transplant team attested to the medical suitability of both donor and recipient. Additionally, laparoscopic nephrectomy now accounts for 50% of the donor nephrectomy procedures done in the United States. With this procedure, hospital stays are brief and perioperative mortality reported for living kidney donors including both open and laparoscopic methods is 0.03%. Therefore, it is a safe procedure for the donor to undertake.

One major ethical principle relevant to this case is beneficence—prevent harm, remove harm, and do good. In this case, all three of these aspects are present. The potential donor prevents harm to the recipient by removing the specter of untimely death and hence removes harm by circumventing the diseased kidney. Therefore, by definition, he is doing good by the act of donation. Although in and out of police custody, the potential donor was able to exert his autonomy, become aware of the risks involved, and agree to give his kidney. The potential donor entered this project fully informed of its risks and potential hazards for both himself and his friend.

Importantly, even though prisoners are relieved of certain civil rights, they are not "owned" body and soul by the state. Prisoners still possess the autonomy to make certain decisions. Through organ donation, prisoners can preserve a sense of self worth and dignity which could become part of their rehabilitation as an offender against society.

Another subtle psychological issue that is raised in this case is the possibility of secondary gain. For the prisoner, the facts suggest no indication of secondary gain in terms of being released or privileged in jail or prison. The prisoner was released from the Louisiana parish jail and the charges were dismissed prior to any decision regarding his suitability as an organ donor. The Tennessee courts expected him to return to their jurisdiction for arraignment following resolution of the organ donation question. Therefore, there was no indication of secondary gain through the judicial system. The only level of secondary gain that seemed to exist was the pleasure of giving a gift, in this case his kidney, so that a friend might live. The ability and willingness to give the gift of life to someone is fundamental to ethical and religious traditions throughout the world. If this level of secondary gain is prohibited in this and similar cases, the social consequences become enormous, affecting the whole of voluntarism that has proved to be such a benefit in the wake of natural disasters, among other things, experienced worldwide throughout history.

So what was the "right" answer in this case? In this particular case, we determined that there were no ethical or legal issues prohibiting the donation to take place. Autonomy, beneficence, legality, morality, and gifting in friendship were all consistent with the notion that the donation could go forward. Individuals, regardless of their standing within society, have the ultimate privilege and responsibility of making decisions that affect the well being and life of others. This case highlights the basic transcultural principle; to do unto others as you would have others do unto you.

References

1. Tendler MD. Medical ethics and Torah morality. In: Carmell A, Domb C, editors. *Challenge: Torah Views on Science and Its Problems*. New York, NY: Feldheim Publishers;1978:492–499.
2. Cohen CB. Public policy and the sale of human organs. *Kennedy Inst Ethics J* 2002;12:47–64.
3. Delmonico FL, Arnold R, Scheper-Hughes N, et al. Ethical incentives, not payment, for organ donation. *New Engl J Med* 2002;346:2002–2005.
4. Bagheri A. Compensated kidney donation: an ethical review of the Iranian model. *Kennedy Inst Ethics J* 2006;16:269–282.
5. Healy GW. Moral and legal aspects of transplantation: prisoners or death convicts as donors. *Transplatation Proc* 1998;30:3653–3654.
6. Curtis AS. Congress considers incentives for organ procurement. *Kennedy Inst Ethics J* 2003;13:51–52.
7. Abecassis M. Consensus statement on the live organ donor. *JAMA* 2000;284:2919–2926.
8. Castro LD. Human organs from prisoners: kidneys for life. *J Med Ethics* 2003;29:171–175.
9. Davis CL, Delmonico FL. Living-donor kidney transplantation: a review of the current practices for the live donor. *J Am Soc Nephrology* 2005;16:2098–2110.

"Coerced donation puts the United States in company with the People's Republic of China."

Forcing Prisoners to Donate Organs as a Condition for Release Is Unethical

St. Louis Post-Dispatch

In the following viewpoint, the editorial board of the St. Louis Post-Dispatch *asserts that prisoners should not be compelled to donate organs as a condition for early release. The board cites the case of sisters Gladys and Jamie Scott, who were granted early release from a Mississippi prison if Gladys donated a kidney to her sister. The board contends that placing such a condition on prisoners is unethical, because it could lead to widespread abuse and be particularly coercive to poor and minority prisoners. The* St. Louis Post-Dispatch *is a major newspaper in St. Louis, Missouri. It is one of the largest newspapers in the Midwest.*

As you read, consider the following questions:

1. As stated by the editorial board, how much did the Scott sisters net in the armed robbery for which they received life sentences?

2. Why are minorities often reluctant to undergo organ transplants, according to the author?

3. As explained by the editorial board, why is an ethics committee from the United Network for Organ Sharing concerned about prisoners donating organs?

Gladys Scott is being forced to donate a kidney as a condition of her early release from prison.

Just before the close of 2010, Mississippi Gov. Haley Barbour granted an early prison release to a pair of sisters serving two life sentences each for an armed robbery that netted $11.

An Early, but Unethical Release

It wasn't just the long-overdue release of Gladys Scott and Jamie Scott that has drawn national attention. Rather, it was the unusual nature of their conviction and the barbaric, unethical condition for their release.

The Scott sisters, neither of whom had prior criminal convictions, were sentenced to two life terms each for a robbery in which no one was seriously injured. They were not alleged to have used force or a weapon; they were charged with luring two men to a place where they were robbed.

As an official condition of their release, 36-year-old Gladys Scott will be required to "donate" a kidney to 38-year-old Jamie Scott, whose kidneys have failed.

Jamie Scott now receives daily dialysis at a cost to the state of about $200,000 a year. Mr. Barbour, a former lobbyist who is considering a run for president in 2012, cited the cost of that treatment in a statement announcing their early release.

The NAACP campaigned to win the sisters' release from what it argued—with strong justification—are unreasonably harsh prison sentences.

Requiring Prisoners to Donate Organs Violates Human Rights

While donating a kidney is extremely safe when donors are healthy and a rigorous evaluation has taken place, it does have a small risk of death. Requiring a prisoner to agree to take this risk in return for parole violates international transplant standards and human rights. The idea that prisoners are able to consent to risky medical treatment in return for benefits is one that ethicists have long questioned.

Frances Kissling, "How Haley Babour's Freedom-For-Kidney-Deal for Scott Sisters Makes U.S. Like China," www.alternet.com, January 7, 2011.

There Is Potential for Widespread Abuse

A spokesman for the Scotts told the *Washington Post* that requiring the organ donation as a condition of release was Gladys Scott's idea.

Mr. Barbour said that the offer to "donate" a kidney, which was contained in an application for early release sent to the governor's office, bolstered their appeal.

No matter who broached the idea first, making it a condition of early release is barbaric and unethical. It sets the stage for even more widespread abuse.

It's not uncommon for convicts facing long prison terms to offer to "donate" organs in return for a lighter sentence.

Such proposals have been widely circulated in recent years as the shortage of transplantable organs, especially kidneys, has grown worse.

More than 110,000 people were awaiting transplants as of Monday afternoon [January 2011]; about 88,000 of them were waiting for a kidney.

African-Americans are disproportionately represented on waiting lists for kidneys, just as they are in prison and on death row.

Minorities, especially African-Americans, wait longer for available organs and often experience worse outcomes.

Part of the reason is that more are uninsured. But many also are reluctant to undergo treatments like organ transplants. That's part of the lingering legacy of the Tuskegee study, in which African-American men who thought they were receiving care became unwitting subjects of a medical experiment.

Letting Prisoners Donate Organs Would Be Coercive

An ethics committee from the United Network for Organ Sharing, which manages the nation's transplant system, raised concerns about allowing prisoners, especially those facing death, reduced sentences in return for "donating" an organ.

The inconsistent ways the death penalty and life sentences are applied "suggest that these proposals would be coercive to particular classes of individuals—minorities and the poor," the committee wrote.

Coerced donation puts the United States in company with the People's Republic of China, the only other nation that makes the organs of prisoners available for transplantation. That's not company we want to keep.

For the sake of the Scott sisters and his own state's humanity, Mr. Barbour should rescind his barbaric edict and issue another one not conditioned on organ donation.

"Creating a savior sibling is a direct violation of the dignity of that person."

The Use of Children as Sibling Donors Is Unethical

Jennifer Lahl

"Savior siblings" are children created via in vitro fertilization to become a match for a brother or sister in need of a donor. In the following viewpoint, Jennifer Lahl argues that this process is immoral. According to Lahl, the process of creating a matching embryo is a form of eugenics that leads to the discarding of less-desirable embryos. She also argues that savior siblings, unlike most organ donors, are not making the decision freely. Lahl is the president of the Center for Bioethics and Culture, an organization that facilitates conversations on issues relating to medicine, science and technology, and other bioethical matters.

As you read, consider the following questions:

1. According to Lahl, why was Adam Nash born?
2. How many embryos did the Nash family create, as stated by the author?
3. What ethical line does Lahl assert has been crossed in the creation of savior siblings?

What does it say about a society which permits, no, which condones the use of medicine and technology for the sole purpose of creating human life just to destroy it? It says we are the culture that has morally and tragically lost its way.

My Sister's Keeper, Jodi Picoult's 2004 novel, just came out on the big screen. Joining other profoundly bioethical films such as *Gattaca* (1997; addresses genetic engineering of super humans), *Million Dollar Baby* (2004; tackles assisted dying), and *The Island* (2005; deals with the creation of human clones to be spare parts for the wealthy sick), *My Sister's Keeper* takes on a real-life issue commonly known as "savior sibling."

How Savior Siblings Are Created

A "savior sibling" refers to the creation of a genetically matched human being, in order to be the savior of a sick child in need of a donor. This requires creating human embryos *in vitro*, which literally means "in glass" (i.e. a test tube), using the egg from the mother and fertilizing the egg with the father's sperm. Then, using pre-implantation technology, the embryos are tested, and the one deemed genetically compatible is implanted into the mother's womb in order for the embryo to grow and develop. Once that baby is delivered, the cord blood is often collected because it provides a perfect match for the sick sibling. Later on, bone marrow, blood, or even organs, can also be taken and used for transplantation for the sick sibling.

Savior siblings are already a reality, and the use of such practices in the United States is not prohibited. Adam Nash was the first savior sibling in the U.S. Adam was born in 2000 to rescue his sister Mollie, who was diagnosed with Fanconi's anemia. Mollie would have otherwise succumbed to death if not for a matched donor. The Nashes created 30 embryos and went through four rounds of in vitro fertilization (IVF) to finally produce Adam, who was the match Mollie needed. Of course, the ethics of the disposition of the 29 other embryos is quite problematic. Adam was chosen, 29 other human lives were not, simply because their DNA was not able to rescue Mollie from a deadly diagnosis.

In Picoult's story, the film opens with a voice-over narration of Anna Fitzgerald, the savior sibling. Anna describes herself as a "designer baby." Note to self—Beware of euphemisms. Euphemisms are rampant in the world of IVF. Selective reduction refers to a situation in which many embryos are transferred into a mother's womb, and then if too many of them implant, the physician, (with the parents' consent), removes the "extra" embryos. Although the removed embryos die because a lethal dose of potassium chloride is injected into the fetal heart, we politely talk about *selective* reductions. Family balancing, social sex-selection and gender selection are terms used to discuss the use of these technologies to intentionally select your children based on their sex and your preference for a boy or a girl. Of course, these euphemistic phrases are used to play down the fact that people are ordering—that is, shopping for—their children purely based on parents' desires. If you want a boy, you screen the embryos, select the male embryo, and discard the female ones in order to "balance" your family. Heaven forbid we should have unbalanced families! The practice of social sex-selection is banned in Canada, so Canadians who wish to order the sex of their children come to the U.S. Social sex-selection is just another euphemism with deadly ramifications. Healthy babies discarded because they are the wrong sex? Surely these are symptoms of a culture in decline!

The Emergence of High-Tech Eugenics

Anna Fitzgerald, the self-described designer baby in Picoult's story—designer not as in Prada, or Coach, or Gucci, but more or less like a cafeteria-style menu selection—was designed for the purpose of being the donor for her sister, Kate. Kate, diagnosed as a young child with leukemia, needs a bone marrow transplant, but NOD[1] is not conventional. . . . Most babies born are unwanted; [Anna] at least was a wanted child. But she is wanted as a product; as a medical treatment; as a donor. Actually, the most recent statistics, taken from a study done in 2001, show that overall 49 percent of babies born in the U.S. are from unintended pregnancies. After that report came out, steps were taken to reduce that number to 30 percent by 2010. We shall see how successful the educational efforts have been when the next report comes out. But of course, as all studies of this nature go, the actual statistics break out quite differently when looked at from educational, economic and age categories.

Also, Anna is not quite accurate in her description of how she was made. She suggests that the doctors took the best part of her mom's DNA and the best part of her dad's DNA and voila—the perfect match was made. If we as a society are going to be able to have an earnest conversation on the ethics of creating savior siblings, we must be intellectually honest with the facts and accuracy of the procedure. Embryos—as in *multiple* embryos, were created, and then tested, and only the one that would provide the genetic match was brought to term. The other embryos were discarded. As was the case with the Nash family, 30 embryos were created and only Adam was selected. This is high-tech eugenics: being selected only because of your "good" genes or being destined for demise because you had the wrong or "bad" genetic make-up.

From this point on, the film does a good job of addressing some real issues head on, showing the complexity of the ethical realities, while fortunately not leaving the audience with a romanticized "happily ever after" ending.

The film poignantly shows the absolute devastation parents face when told that their child has a dreadful disease that will most likely kill her. There is no sugar coating of the stress that is placed on a marriage or other children in the family, and the strained family dynamics when a child is seriously or chronically ill. That means gut-wrenching decisions, and the constant suggestion that all hope is lost and all you have to grasp for are straws.

The film deals directly with Anna's life and experience, as she has lived it knowing that she is a product who only exists because someone else desperately needed her—or parts of her at least.

"Congratulations! It's a saviour sibling," cartoon by Grizelda. www.cartoonstock.com.

Creating People as a Means to an End

And here is the heart of the ethical matter at hand. Technology, apart from any ethical or moral compass, has progressed to the point where, for the first time in history, we are able to intentionally create human life and allow it to fully develop solely because we need that life to save another. And perhaps even more worrisome is the reality that other lives were created, and then destroyed because it did not perfectly meet the need of another.

119

Realistically, there could be several embryos which provided the genetic match, but since only one is needed; even embryos which make the cut are discarded. In our desire to relieve suffering, to seek healing and cures, and to avoid death, we have crossed a bright ethical line by seeking to use one human life for the good of another.

Whether we look for moral guidance from our religious texts or to secular historical documents, it is important that we as a society remain rooted in the belief in the inherent dignity of all persons. The U.N. Declaration on Human Rights warns that wherever there is "disregard and contempt for human rights," "barbarous acts" are sure to follow. Surely, the rights of the savior sibling have been denied when from their first breath they are being used as a means to an end. The World Medical Declaration of Helsinki claims that, "the duty of the physician is to promote and safeguard the health of patients." Isn't there an immediate conflict of interest between the doctor and the patient, not to mention the savior sibling, who has nothing to gain, but perhaps is exposed to medical risk while not even being a patient? Organ donation is perhaps one of the greatest altruistic deeds a person can do. But in organ donation, the gift is freely given. It is never taken, coerced or bought. Creating a savior sibling is a direct violation of the dignity of that person. It treats human life as something to be made, manufactured and used as a commodity.

Early in the film, Anna hires an attorney and announces, "I want to sue my parents for the rights to my own body." From the moment of birth, the savior sibling has been denied the full rights to her own body, and to willingly and freely be her sister's keeper.

Note

1. Nucleotide-binding oligomerization domain (NOD) deficiency is linked to various autoimmune diseases such as leukemia.

"Parents have kids for all sorts of reasons. . . . Are these [reasons] inherently more ethically sound than the idea of a 'saviour sibling'?"

Concerns About Savior Siblings Should Be Based on Facts

Erin Nelson and Timothy Caulfield

In the following viewpoint, Erin Nelson and Timothy Caulfield argue that discussions about the ethics of "savior siblings" should be based on facts. According to the authors, the debate over the issue ignores the laws that govern organ donation in the United States, Canada, and Great Britain. The authors further point out that donation of umbilical cord blood causes no harm to a newborn donor, and society cannot judge whether having a child that is a perfect donor match for an older sibling is a less valid reason for having a child. Nelson is a research fellow at the University of Alberta's Health Law Institute, and Caulfield is the Canada research chair in health law and policy and a research director at the institute.

As you read, consider the following questions:

1. As stated by the authors, under what circumstance does the Human Fertilization and Embryology Authority permit the selection of embryos?
2. Why do Nelson and Caulfield have mixed feelings about popular portrayals of medical ethics?
3. What is the Canadian law that gives the federal government jurisdiction over reproductive technology, according to the authors?

The debate over embryo selection is going to heat up again with tomorrow's [June 2009] opening of *My Sister's Keeper.* The film depicts the story of a young girl who is the product of pre-implantation genetic diagnosis. She was selected as an embryo by her parents because she is a perfect genetic match for her older sister, who suffers from leukemia. She is, in other words, a "saviour sibling."

Selecting Embryos to Create Donors

The debate around saviour siblings (and designer babies) flared with particular heat in England several years ago. Two families asked the Human Fertilisation and Embryology Authority (HFEA) for permission to select embryos that were perfect tissue matches for older siblings who suffered from blood disorders. Only one family was granted permission; the second sought treatment in the United States, and the older sibling now appears cured of Diamond-Blackfan anemia. The first family, after a court battle between the HFEA and an organization called Comment on Reproductive Ethics, eventually tried to use various reproductive technologies to create a cord blood donor sibling, but without success.

Since these cases, the HFEA has revised its views and now clearly permits the selection of embryos that may lead to the birth of a child who can provide compatible tissue "for the treatment of an existing child who is affected by a serious or life-threatening condition."

The parents in the British cases were seeking a tissue-matched cord blood donor. Umbilical cord blood is a rich source of stem cells that can produce all types of blood cells and thus can treat and potentially cure many types of blood disorders, including blood cancers such as leukemia. Cord blood is usually discarded at birth. There is no risk of harm to a newborn cord blood donor.

In the book on which *My Sister's Keeper* is based, the parents sought a cord blood donor for their daughter. But as time goes on, Anna, the "saviour sibling," undergoes more and more invasive procedures to help her sister. Ultimately, she is told by her parents that she will need to donate a kidney to save her sister's life.

There Is a Distorted Portrayal of Legal Issues

As academics, we have mixed feelings about popular and media portrayals of complex issues in health law and ethics. On the one hand, public conversation about ethical and legal issues is essential and can further sound public policy. And popular media can provide an ideal vehicle to engage the public. On the other hand, it is too easy for issues to be distorted in such a way as to derail that useful conversation.

My Sister's Keeper is a perfect example of the latter. The very idea that parents are free to decide that one of their children could be forced to donate an organ to a sibling is foreign to Canadian law. There is no way that a cord blood donor could become an organ donor simply based on parental desires. In Canada, living organ donation is governed by provincial and territorial laws that require consent from the donor, and that (for the most part) preclude living donation by minors. Even in the United States, where minors can be living organ donors, we would be shocked to see a court decide—over the objections of the potential donor—that a child should undergo unnecessary surgery solely for the benefit of someone else.

Savior Siblings Are Valued

The donor or savior sibling seems, at first blush, to be the only party in whom the burdens might outweigh the benefits. Granted they are "selected" because of their potential to help their sibling, but are also more likely than the average newborn to be free of discoverable genetic disease. There is no evidence that they are less valued than other children in the family and one could imagine them being more valued. There are no reports that savior children are wanted or valued only because of their role as rescuers.

Peter C. Williams, "Saviors as Saints or Sinners?," Pediatric Transplantation, *2008.*

But these issues, no doubt, will be the focus of the ethical debate that will surface in the wake of the movie's release.

The sensationalized portrayal of the legal issues also makes a consideration of the central ethical question—the moral acceptability of "designer" babies—more difficult to consider in a rational manner. Parents have kids for all sorts of reasons. Some are looking for a hockey star. Others need children to work in the fields or for long-term security. Still others have children by accident. Are these, or the myriad other reasons, inherently more ethically sound than the idea of a "saviour sibling"?

The Debate Should Be Based on Facts

In Canada, the Assisted Human Reproduction Act gives the federal government jurisdiction to oversee reproductive technologies, leaving it free to decide whether saviour siblings should be allowed in this country. As parents, we are both grateful that this debate remains in the realm of the hypothetical. But we also feel deep empathy for those parents who find themselves in a situation that leads them to consider these options.

We hope the movie stirs interest in these issues, but public debate should be informed by the facts—both scientific and legal.

Periodical and Internet Sources
Bibliography

The following articles have been selected to supplement the diverse views presented in this chapter.

Lindsay Abrams	"Could You Love Someone Without a Face? Making Facial Transplants Common Practice," *The Atlantic*, September 10, 2012.
John L. Allen	"The Nightmare Scenario of Organ Donation," *National Catholic Reporter*, November 16, 2007.
Hannah Beech	"Are Executed Prisoners' Organs Still Being Harvested in China?," *Time*, June 7, 2011.
The Economist	"O Death, When Is Thy Sting? Defining Death," October 4, 2008.
Maggie Fazeli Fard	"Face Transplant for Virginia Man Is Lauded as Most Extensive in History," *Washington Post*, March 27, 2012.
Raffi Khatchadourian	"Transfiguration," *New Yorker*, February 13, 2012.
Sarah Levitt	"Saviour Siblings: Genetic Screening and Policy," *The Meducator*, vol. 1, 2008.
Bohdan Pomahac, et al.	"Three Patients with Full Facial Transplantation," *New England Journal of Medicine*, February 23, 2012.
Darshak Sanghavi	"When Does Death Start?," *New York Times Magazine*, December 16, 2009.
Dick Teresi, interviewed by Brian Bethune	"On the Debate over When Life Really Ends, and the Possibility Cadavers Can Feel Pain," *Maclean's*, March 19, 2012.
Stephanie Warren	"The Face of Progress," *Science World*, November 14, 2011.

What Is the Future of Organ Donation?

Chapter Preface

Patients who are ineligible for a heart transplant or are on a delayed waiting list may receive a total artificial heart (TAH) as an alternative. TAHs are devices that replace the two lower chambers, or ventricles, of the heart. The first use of an artificial heart for a patient waiting for a transplant was in 1969. However, that patient only lived a combined ninety-six hours with the artificial heart and the transplanted heart. In 1982, what can be considered the first genuine success occurred when Barney Clark survived for 112 days on a Jarvik-7 artificial heart.

As of late 2012, two types of artificial hearts are currently in use in the United States with US Food and Drug Administration approval. The AbioCor is restricted to patients who are ineligible for transplants. The other artificial heart is the CardioWest TAH-t, which is approved both as an alternative to a donor heart and as a bridge to transplantation. A study in the *New England Journal of Medicine* found that the one-year survival rate of patients who received the CardioWest artificial heart was 70 percent, compared to a 31 percent survival rate for patients who did not get that implant. In addition, for patients who later received a donor heart, the one- and five-year survival rates were 86 percent and 64 percent, respectively, compared to 84 percent and 69 percent for patients who had a heart transplant without first getting a TAH.

The prospects for TAHs continue to improve. A French company, Carmat, is developing an artificial heart that could be available in Europe by 2013. According to Bruce Crumley, writing for *Time* magazine, this artificial heart more accurately mimics a real heart by using two pumps instead of one. If successful, this new device could save thousands of lives each year. As Crumley explains, "an estimated 20,000 people worldwide... are each year in urgent need of a heart transplant for survival. Currently, only about a quarter of those patients receive transplanted hearts from donors. The need for a viable artificial alternative is clear."

Whether it's due to the implantation of artificial organs or to technology that has yet to be developed, organ transplants in the coming decades may be vastly different from our current understanding. The authors in the following chapter consider the future of organ donation.

> *"Pig organs have multiple potential advantages over organs derived from brain-dead human donors."*

Xenotransplantation Has Potential

William Edward Beschorner

Xenotransplantation (using organs and tissues from another species) could be a viable solution to the organ shortage, but several barriers must first be addressed, William Edward Beschorner asserts in the following viewpoint. He argues that pig organs in particular offer a variety of advantages, including resistance to human pathogens and the ability to be raised in a controlled environment. However, Beschorner acknowledges, xenotransplantation will not occur on a large scale until the barriers of unrealistic regulation, inadequate funding, and inadequate source herds are addressed. Beschorner was an associate professor of medicine at the Johns Hopkins University School of Medicine.

As you read, consider the following questions:

1. According to Beschorner, in what ways are pig organs similar to human organs?

2. What medical event occurred in 1963, as stated by the author?

3. How could xenotransplantation be combined with stem cell technology, as detailed by Beschorner?

Organ transplantation has been called a victim of its own success. Transplanted human organs can replace failed organs and eliminate the need for insulin administration in patients with insulin-dependent diabetes; however, because of a severe shortage of human donors, less than 1 in 20 individuals who require transplantation are able to undergo the procedure.

Many Patients Are Left Waiting

Patients who require heart transplantation and are designated on the waiting list as 1A priority (urgent) have a life expectancy of less than a week. If they undergo transplantation, they typically experience more than 10 additional years of active life. Less than 2,000 heart transplants are performed annually in the United States. The Organ Procurement and Transplantation Network/ United Network of Organ Sharing (OPTN/UNOS) waiting list has nearly 3,000 heart transplant candidates. However, this barely explains the true need because these are the candidates of highest priority. The International Heart and Lung Transplant society has estimated that more than 50,000 Americans annually could benefit from heart transplantation if donors were available.

For primary organs and tissues, 27,958 organ and tissue transplants were performed in the United States in 2008, excluding corneal transplants. More than 101,000 Americans are currently on the OPTN/UNOS waiting list. As with the hearts, the waiting list greatly underestimates the true need. For hearts, kidneys, livers, and pancreatic islets, approximately 500,000 transplants or more could be performed annually in the United States and more than 1.3 million transplants could be performed annually in the developed world if organs were available.

Pig Organs Have Potential

Although stem cell technology and tissue engineering are potential solutions to the organ shortage, xenotransplantation (transplanting organs and tissues from a different species) has generated considerable interest as a potential solution. Pigs are considered the optimal source of xenotransplant organs. Many pig organs are similar to the human counterparts in size, anatomy, and physiology. Large numbers of pigs can be quickly produced under standardized clean conditions. Pigs can be readily modified. Genes can be added or removed. Human cells can be grown in the pig.

Contrary to common belief, pig organs have multiple potential advantages over organs derived from brain-dead human donors. With human organs, little can be done before the donor is declared brain dead. After brain death, organs are procured in an emergency manner and are immediately transported to the medical center performing the transplant. The transplant is also performed with little warning. The transplant organ may come from a suboptimal donor with advanced age and chronic medical conditions or from a carrier with undetected infectious agents or malignant cells. A donor pig is raised under controlled conditions, specifically for use as an organ donor. Potential pathogens can be eliminated from the herd. The donor pig can be extensively analyzed. Organs are procured from young, robust donors. In xenotransplants, the procurement and transplant is performed on a scheduled elective basis.

Xenografts may provide medical advantages as well. These grafts are resistant to many human pathogens specific to human tissues, such as HIV, hepatitis, and human cytomegalovirus. Tumors such as melanoma have also been transferred to the recipient through human allografts. Pigs can be produced that are free of potential pathogens. Xenografts may be resistant to autoimmune reactions, such as the autoimmune destruction of beta cells with type 1 diabetes.

Despite these advantages, relatively few xenotransplants have been successfully performed in experimental models and none have been performed in the clinical arena. This is due to 3 main causes. First, xenotransplantation is subject to severe rejection, involving many different antigen disparities between humans and pigs that elicit multiple mechanisms of immune rejection. Current opinion dictates that severe immune suppression is required to prevent rejection, and this subjects the recipient to a high risk of infection and toxicity. Second, the perceived need for increased immune suppression leads to concern about infectious agents from the pig, including exogenous viruses (e.g., circoviruses, hepatitis E) and endogenous viruses (e.g., porcine endogenous retrovirus [PERV], which may lead to novel infectious diseases in humans (i.e., xenozoonoses). Third, for some tissues such as the liver, the physiological function of the pig organ is insufficiently close to the human to provide long-term support.

Fortunately, significant progress has been made on all fronts. Several xenotransplant technologies are now in clinical trials. . . .

Xenotransplantation Is Not a New Concept

The use of animals as organ and tissue donors is not a new idea. At a time when medical technology and understanding of immunology and physiology were primitive, animals were the preferred source.

Jean-Babtiste Denys performed the first blood transfusion into a patient in 1667 using blood taken from a sheep. In 1906, [M.] Jaboulay performed the first vascular xenotransplants, transplanting kidneys from a pig and a dog into patients with renal insufficiency. In 1963, [C.R.] Hitchcock transplanted a kidney from a baboon into 65-year-old woman; it functioned for 4 days. [K.] Reemtsma and [T.E.] Starzl achieved a measure of clinical success transplanting kidneys from nonhuman primates into human recipients.

However, over the next 25 years, focus turned to transplanting organs and tissues from human donors. In the early 1990s, porcine islets prepared from fetal pigs were transplanted into diabetic patients with modest immune suppression. Porcine C-peptide was monitored in the urine until the grafts eventually rejected. In 1992 and 1993, 2 orthotopic xenotransplants were performed placing baboon livers into patients with liver failure related to hepatitis B virus infection. Multidrug therapy was administered to prevent cellular and antibody-mediated rejection. The patients survived 70 and 26 days, respectively. The grafts provided at least partial function. Although the grafts did not undergo rejection, one of the patients developed a terminal aspergillosis related to the immune suppression.

Baboon marrow was transplanted into a patient with AIDS with the knowledge that the baboon $CD4^+$ lymphocytes were resistant to HIV. Although the patient rejected the baboon cells, his clinical condition improved, and he continued to do well at the time of publication [January 14, 2010].

Dopaminergic neurons from a fetal pig were transplanted into the brain of a patient with Parkinson's disease. The transplant significantly improved the clinical course of the patient. Seven months later, the fetal pig neurons were identified. The implantation of pig neural tissue into an immune privileged environment of the brain reduced the risk of rejection. Unfortunately, a subsequent controlled trial failed to demonstrate a statistically significant difference with the control group.

Patients in acute liver failure have been supported for a few hours to days with extracorporeal liver perfusion (ECLP) while a human liver donor is sought. Blood from the patient is perfused through the pig liver and returned. These procedures indicate that the pig liver is functional on a short-term basis. Patients typically show clinical improvement with reduction of blood ammonia and lactic acid levels, conjugation and excretion of bilirubin, and stabilization of prothrombin time.

Devices that incorporate cells or tissue from animals or incorporate human cells or tissues that have been cocultured with animal cells are considered xenografts. One promising device provides short-term support for patients with acute liver failure.

Initial clinical trials were promising, providing time to bridge to a human liver transplant. Others showed spontaneous recovery during the support period.

Following a series of public hearings by the National Institutes of Health (NIH), the Centers for Disease Control and Prevention (CDC), and the FDA [Food and Drug Administration], the FDA published guidelines for xenotransplantation to address concerns raised about infectious diseases from donor animals. The latest guidelines were published in 2003. For a clinical trial to be allowed, the investigator must demonstrate evidence of efficacy of the xenotransplants in nonhuman primates. The investigator must also demonstrate compliance with the safety guidelines, including a certified source herd, prolonged archiving of tissues and records, and current good manufacturing practice (cGMP) facilities and procedures.

Most likely, the first successful clinical trials will be with cellular transplants, such as pancreatic islets, neural cells, or hepatocytes. Because vascular xenografts are sensitive to rejection of the endothelial cells, the threshold is set higher. Heart xenografts and kidney xenografts will likely be the first tested. Lung xenografts are presently the most challenging xenografts because of the extensive capillary network and sensitivity of endothelial cells to hyperacute rejection.

Regenerative medicine urgently needs an alternative technology to supplement the transplantation of human allografts for the cure of organ and tissue failure. The leading technologies to provide tissues and organs include xenotransplantation, stem cell technology, and tissue engineering. Xenotransplantation is the first such technology to be pursued and the most advanced. . . .

There Are Barriers to Large-Scale Applications

The large-scale clinical application of xenotransplantation is threatened by 3 fiscal and logistical barriers: unrealistic federal

The Risk of Xenotransplantation Cannot Be Completely Eliminated

Risk will be an unavoidable artifact of xenotransplantation research. We cannot be rid of it and neither can we minimize it in order to optimize a xenotransplantation product's level of safety. If we place the burden of safety optimization on xenotransplantation, we will never reap any of its potential benefits. From a traditionally rational perspective, laboratory research would continue ad infinitum because increasing safety will always be the more rational choice procedure. However, what immediately strikes me as irrational in this behavior is the lack of any clearly defined stopping point for one's inquiry, the incessant insistence on the better option. This method of decision-making offers no point at which laboratory research can cease and clinical trials may commence, and is thus of no pragmatic use to us.

Ololade Olakanmi, "Xenotransplantation:
A Rational Choice?," Penn Bioethics Journal,
vol. 2, no. 2, Spring 2006.

regulation, inadequate funding by industry and government, and inadequate qualified source herds of clean swine.

The federal guidelines that regulate xenotransplantation were formed following workshops that were concerned about the potential public health hazards of zoonotic infections, particularly concern about the potential threat of PERV. At the time of those discussions, prolonged acceptance of pig xenografts in preclinical studies could be achieved only with high doses of antirejection drugs. Speculation held that if xenotransplantation was performed on a large scale, recombination of the PERV subtypes could lead to a new virus that was contagious, pathological, and a threat to the public health. The resulting guidelines called for patient followup for as long as 50 years and severe restrictions on xenograft recipients, such as travel. Although the guidelines were appropriate for the information at that time, they unfortunately discouraged large pharmaceutical and medical device companies from investing in xenotransplantation.

In addition to the stringent requirements for monitoring recipients, companies were concerned about the liability of pursuing a technology perceived to be a potential hazard to the public health. However, since PERV was initially described, numerous studies have shown no evidence of PERV becoming contagious or being pathological. Many strains fail to pass PERV to human cells in coculture. The molecular virology of PERV passage is now understood. Swine strains have been produced that are free of the PERV-C that is needed for passage. Indeed, in the near future, swine strains will likely be produced with no genomic PERV.

The risk of a public health hazard from PERV needs to be re-examined in light of current information and developments. The risk of a public health hazard from PERV in pigs is not measurably greater than a public health hazard from technologies based on human cells and tissues. Indeed, the risk for transmitting exogenous pathogens such as hepatitis, HIV, and malignant cells to patients is much less for porcine xenografts than with human based transplants. One could speculate that some unknown virus or mutational event could still produce a public health hazard. Totally ruling out the unknown is impossible. Fear of the unknown, however, is irrational and effectively blocks all technological development. Should blood transfusions and human tissue transplants also be severely restricted because of this unknown factor? The infinitesimal risk of the unknown must be balanced against the tremendous potential for regenerative medicine.

The second barrier is lack of funding. Although xenotransplantation is the closest to clinical reality of the 3 major regenerative technologies, it is also the least-supported technology.

Large corporations have ceased their support of xenotransplantation. The NIH supports xenotransplantation at a level far below that for stem cell and tissue engineering. For example, the recent economic stimulation package (American Recovery and Reinvestment Act of 2009) provided $200 million for 200 challenge grants. Although multiple challenge topics address issues with stem cell and tissue-engineering technology, no challenges are posted for improving xenotransplantation. As stem cell and tissue engineering are at a speculative stage of development with major technical hurdles to overcome, abandoning xenotransplantation, which is at an advanced stage of development, is absurd.

The third major barrier to xenotransplantation is lack of sufficient qualified source herds. At this time, only a handful of swine herds are qualified to be used for clinical trials. All of these are small herds with less than 100 pigs. Several small clinical trials are currently being pursued. The likelihood that at least one of these trials will be successful and lead to a new device approval is great. However, when such approval is achieved, not nearly enough qualified pigs will be available to satisfy the unmet need. Maintaining and developing qualified herds with the appropriate barrier facilities and husbandry is very expensive. The current herds need to be greatly expanded for widespread clinical application. This will take several years and much more support.

Regrettably, the 3 regenerative medicine technologies are usually considered in competition with each other. The underlying assumption is that one will "win" and become the standard technology for alternate tissues whereas the others will "lose" and be abandoned. Considering the enormity of the unmet need in regenerative medicine, this assumption is unfortunate. Most likely, each technology will prove to be optimal for different select diseases.

The Potential for Hybrid Technologies

A more promising approach would be to combine these technologies. Xenotransplantation could provide a cost-effective and sterile bioreactor for maturing stem cells into tissues that can be transplanted. Xenotransplantation could also provide the scaffolding for tissue engineering.

Several developments in recent years support such hybrid technologies.

Our program has been growing human hematopoietic lymphocytes and stem cells from the transplant recipient, with the goal of producing human antigen-specific T-regulatory cells that prevent rejection of pig xenografts after transfer from the chimeric pig back into the recipient. Prolonged survival and function of pig islet cell clusters has been realized in nonhuman primates without posttransplant immune suppression.

As an example, the pig liver differs from human livers in several critical aspects. Although pig livers have provided short-term life support, they are unlikely to be effective for long-term support. Human hepatocytes grow within the fetal pig liver and demonstrate normal sinusoidal architecture. Expansion is limited though by competition by the native pig hepatocytes. Transgenic pigs have been produced that express suicide genes (thymidine kinase or cytosine deaminase) in the pig hepatocytes. By providing the chimeric pig with a prodrug such as ganciclovir for thymidine kinase, selectively and conditionally destroying the pig hepatocytes is possible, giving the human hepatocytes an edge to expand.

Human hepatocytes may not be essential to develop hybrid livers. For example, when fetal lambs were injected with human CD34-positive bone marrow cells, the livers of the newborn lambs were shown to contain human hepatocytes.

With stem cell technology, the pluripotent stem cells would not be directly transplanted into the recipient because of the risk of developing teratomas. The challenge has been to differentiate the stem cells outside of the patient. Although the production of human islets or insulin producing glucose sensitive beta cells remains a challenge, the transplantation of pancreatic primordia can provide good glucose control to diabetic recipients. Fetal pigs could be used as a cost effective bioreactor to expand human stem cells or primordia and differentiate them into mature beta cells or islets. . . .

With sufficient support, xenotransplantation will address the large unmet need for many of the diseases requiring replacement of failed tissues and organs. In some devices, xenotransplantation may be a stand-alone technology. In other technologies, it may be combined with stem cell or tissue engineering technology. The future of xenotransplantation and regenerative medicine could potentially be very exciting.

"*Consent of an individual to a
xenotransplant has significant bearing
on the protection of society.*"

Ethical Debate: Ethics of Xeno-Transplantation

Murali Krishna and Peter Lepping

*In the following viewpoint, Murali Krishna and Peter Lepping
opine that xenotransplantation—using an organ from an animal, typically a pig—is not the right answer to the organ shortage.
Krishna and Lepping assert that even though xenotransplantation
may save lives, the risk of infections and the need for long-term immunosuppressant therapy could greatly reduce the patient's quality
of life. In addition to the impacts xenotransplantation might have
on the individual, the authors also argue that the effects on society
as well as the rights of animals must be considered. Krishna is a
consultant psychiatrist at CSI Holdsworth Memorial Hospital in
Mysore, India, and Lepping is a visiting professor in psychiatry at
Glyndçr University in Wrexham, North Wales.*

As you read, consider the following questions:

1. What are allotransplantations, as defined by Krishna and
   Lepping?

2. In the view of the authors, what steps would be necessary to produce pathogen-free donor organs?

3. How might Muslims and Jews respond to xenotransplantations, according to the authors?

Interest in cross-species transplantation has recently been re-kindled.[1] This is due to many developments including the shortage of donor organs, advances in transplant medicine, investment in biotechnology research, and the non-availability of more ethically suitable alternatives to human organs.[1,2] Increasing success rates in allotransplantations (organs from different member of the same species) has increased the demand on donor organs. Other types of transplantation include autotransplants (a person's own organs or tissues are used for transplantation) and isotransplants (organs from one person are transplanted into another genetically identical person, like an identical twin). These options are limited in terms of body parts used and numbers.

Good facts inform good ethics. It is therefore obligatory to look into the current research knowledge about xenotransplants (organs from one species to another, for example animal to human) in more detail. The advocates of xenotransplantation argue that it could provide organs "relatively quickly" and hence save more lives. If animal organs were easily available for transplantation most eligible recipients would receive the transplantation much earlier on in their illness. It is argued that this may decrease distress and suffering. Whilst xenotransplantation may theoretically increase the survival time, it is unclear, however, whether the negative impact on recipients' quality of life due to long-term immunosuppressant therapy and the risk of zoonotic infections would in fact worsen the overall long-term outcome.[3] Recent research suggests that xenotransplantation may be associated with the transmission of pig microorganisms including viruses, bacteria, fungi, and parasites. Because of the recipient's likely immunosuppressed state, infection and pathologic consequences may be more pronounced. Transmission of most microorganisms with the exception of the porcine endogenous retroviruses may be prevented by screening the donor pig and qualified pathogen-free breeding. However, porcine endogenous retroviruses represent a special risk as they are present in the genome of all pigs and infect human cells in vitro. Until now, no porcine endogenous retrovirus transmission was observed in experimental and clinical xenotransplantations as well as in numerous infection experiments.[4] Nevertheless, strategies need to be developed to prevent their transmission to humans. It is equally possible that many eligible recipients may be denied having a trial of xenotransplantation by doctors who believe that there is in unfavourable risk-benefit ratio. The limited long-term data on outcomes of xenotransplants thus renders ethical analysis difficult.

There is some evidence to suggest that the recipients of animal organ donation may develop a different sell image with possible consequences for their identity.[5,6] This happens with human organs at times, but may be a more significant problem with animal organs, as the recipient knows that they have been given a non-human organ. Loss of identity jeopardises the core principle of autonomy, which underpins all medical treatment.

The risk of zoonosis to the recipient and to the wider society cannot be accurately estimated.[7] Hence there is a requirement for vigilant post-operative monitoring[8] with a possibility of engaging article 5 and 8 of the European Convention of Human Rights (for England and Wales; Human Rights Act 1998).† Article 12 may also be engaged as the recipients may be restricted from having physical relationships, carrying out their routine day to day activities and socialisation. This is because the prevention of possible risk to the wider public from zoonosis may require the recipient to be put under restrictions with regard to their engagement with others. This may include restrictions to go out, which can result into de facto temporary detentions at home. Hence consenting to xeno-transplantation would be "binding

"Animal Transplants," cartoon by Ed Fischer. www.cartoonstock.com.

and contractual" over a long period of time. The subject may not have the right to withdraw. This is entering into a de facto contract with potential restrictions or even deprivation of human rights. This would restrict the ability to give informed consent even for a well informed patient, as it is difficult to be fully appreciative of future restrictions of one's liberty.

Autonomous decision making and thus informed consent may also be put at risk by other factors surrounding xenotransplantation. The decision to embark on xenotransplantation may be primarily driven by an instinctual wish to survive due to a lack of other viable alternatives. Patients in these circumstances may have little or no consideration to medium and long-term effects on themselves and society. However, it is the consideration of such long-term consequences that make a truly autonomous decision, and differentiate it from a decision that is purely based on immediate instinct. Whilst the wish to survive is legitimate it is difficult to make decisions free of the pressure to survive when there is a lack of alternatives.

It also brings up an even more important question: Can any person *ever* consent to a future restriction or deprivation of their liberty or other human rights? Even if there were an option to define acceptable future restrictions it would be likely that patients could still challenge the legality of any such agreements. They could quite reasonably argue that they have agreed to the restrictions under duress because of a lack of viable alternatives to their xeno-transplants.

Xenotransplantation touches questions of utilitarianism (greatest good for the greatest numbers) and public protection.[2] Utilitarianism takes into account the reasonable interests of society in good outcomes, fairness in the distribution of resources, and the prevention of harm to others. The Nuffield council on bio-ethics embraces a utilitarian approach. However, there are limits to the utilitarian argument for xenotransplants. Even if they were widely available, the treatment would be immensely expensive. Production of a pathogen-free donor organ would involve rearing animals in strictly controlled environments, subjecting them to rigorous standards of examination and surveillance. The additional costs of developing a sustainable work force to provide transplantation and post-transplant surveillance of the patient and the community would be high. The insurance providers may not cover expenses of a xenotransplant. Public health care providers may decline to provide this treatment as it may not be recommended by expert groups as cost effective. Xenotransplantation may commence in the developing world where the regulations are lax and the poor can be more easily exploited.[8] Patients who would potentially benefit from xenotransplantation may not be able to afford it due to its cost with serious implications for fairness.

Xenotransplantation also raises other critical questions in relation to the wider community. We have seen that consent of an individual to a xenotransplant has significant bearing on the protection of society.[7] Should the members of a community therefore be consulted if there were any xeno-transplantation experiments in their region? The risk is primarily due to the risk of zoonotic infections, the need for surveillance, and possible quarantine of contacts.[7,9] In addition, if health authorities were to fund expensive experimental interventions like xenotransplantation, other routine treatments of greater potential benefits to society may be jeopardised. Society may also have views about particular animals being used as donor animals.[10] For example religions like Islam and Judaism may feel that pigs are 'ritually unclean'. They may therefore not approve of certain animals to be used for donation, and more worryingly may fail to socially accept recipients with such 'unclean' transplants.[11]

From a deontological perspective (this judges the morality of an action based on the action's adherence to a rule or principle) some authors assert that animals have rights similar to those considered appropriate for humans.[12,13] The protection of animals has legal status in many countries. Consequentialists may view the suffering and death of an animal as acceptable for the betterment of a human patient, as they would judge the morality of an action primarily by its end result. They would argue that potential benefits and improvement in human welfare arising from xenotransplantation may justify the loss of animal life. However, this will never satisfy the animal rights lobby; especially as whilst minimising the risk of acquired infections, the animals have to forgo greater suffering in the form of isolation, monitoring and investigations. Furthermore, genetic modification can have both immediate and long-term negative effects on animals.

In summary, xenotransplantation has significant ethical consequences. On an individual level, there are the questions of pressure to consent that may negate autonomy and the validity of that consent as well as the difficulties that arise when patients are asked to consent to future restrictions of their human rights. On a societal level there are questions of cost and benefit analysis as well as risks from zoonotic infections. In addition, questions of animal rights need to be addressed before any programs are likely to go ahead.

† **Appendix of Articles of the Human Rights Act.**
- Article 8 of the Human Rights Act 1998 (The right to respect for private and family life, home and correspondence)
- Article 5 (The right to liberty)
- Article 12 (The right to marry and found a family)

References

1. Advisory Group on the Ethics of Xenotransplantation: Animal Tissues into Humans. London, Stationery Office, 1997
2. Nuffield Council on Bioethics-Animal-to-Human Transplants: The ethics of xeno-transplantation. London, Nuffield Council on Bioethics, 1996
3. Chapman, L.E.E., Folks, T.M., Salomon, D.R., Paterson, A.P., Eggerman, T.E., Noguchi, P.D.: Xenotransplantation and xenogeneic infections. N. Engl. J. Med. 333: 1498, 1995
4. Denner J.: Infectious risk in xenotransplantation—what post-transplant screening for the human receipient? Xenotransplantation. 2011 May; 18(3):151–7
5. Franklin, P.: Psychological aspects of kidney transplantation and organ donation. In Kidney Transplantation, Principles and Practice (4th ed.), P.J. Morris, editor, Philadelphia, Saunders, pp. 532–541, 1994
6. Nature Biotechnology Editorial P403, 1996
7. Public Health Service: Draft guidelines on infectious disease issues in xenotransplan-tation: Fed. Register 61:49919, 1996
8. Oman Daily Observer: Organ transplant doctor held. January 11, 1997
9 Witt, C.J., Meslin, F-X., Heyman, D.: Emerging and Other Communicable Disease Surveillance and Control (EMC). Draft WHO Recommendations on Xenotransplantation and Infectious Disease Prevention. Geneva, World Health Organization, 1997
10. Institute of Medicine: Xenotransplantation: Science, Ethics and Public Policy. Washington, DC, National Academy Press, 1996
11. Daar, A.S.: Xenotransplantation and Religion: The major monotheistic religions, Xenotransplatation 2(4): 61, 1994
12. Singer, P.: Animal Liberation. New York, Random House, 1975
13. Regan, T.: The case for animal rights. University of California Press, Los Angeles, 1983

> *"Those waiting for transplants are unlikely to worry too much about what replacement body parts look like, so long as they work."*

Artificial Organs Could Save Lives

The Economist

In the following viewpoint, The Economist explains how in the future, people in need of an organ might be able to get an artificial one made by a three-dimensional bio-printer. The printer uses stem cells from adult bone marrow and fat, along with a hydrogel, to create the desired structure. According to the magazine, this technology will first be used to make skin, muscles, and blood vessels but could eventually create more complicated body parts. The Economist is a weekly newspaper that focuses on international politics and business news.

As you read, consider the following questions:

1. What will the bio-printer be able to produce by 2015, according to the magazine?
2. As stated by *The Economist*, how many cells are in the droplets created by the Organovo machine?

3. What features might be missing from a man-made kidney, as stated by the magazine?

The great hope of transplant surgeons is that they will, one day, be able to order replacement body parts on demand. At the moment, a patient may wait months, sometimes years, for an organ from a suitable donor. During that time his condition may worsen. He may even die. The ability to make organs as they are needed would not only relieve suffering but also save lives. And that possibility may be closer with the arrival of the first commercial 3D bio-printer for manufacturing human tissue and organs.

The new machine, which costs around $200,000, has been developed by Organovo, a company in San Diego that specialises in regenerative medicine, and Invetech, an engineering and automation firm in Melbourne, Australia. One of Organovo's founders, Gabor Forgacs of the University of Missouri, developed the prototype on which the new 3D bio-printer is based. The first production models will soon be delivered to research groups which, like Dr. Forgacs's, are studying ways to produce tissue and organs for repair and replacement. At present much of this work is done by hand or by adapting existing instruments and devices.

To start with, only simple tissues, such as skin, muscle and short stretches of blood vessels, will be made, says Keith Murphy, Organovo's chief executive, and these will be for research purposes. Mr. Murphy says, however, that the company expects that within five years, once clinical trials are complete, the printers will produce blood vessels for use as grafts in bypass surgery. With more research it should be possible to produce bigger, more complex body parts. Because the machines have the ability to make branched tubes, the technology could, for example, be used to create the networks of blood vessels needed to sustain larger printed organs, like kidneys, livers and hearts.

How the Printer Works

Organovo's 3D bio-printer works in a similar way to some rapid-prototyping machines used in industry to make parts and mechanically functioning models. These work like inkjet printers, but with a third dimension. Such printers deposit droplets of polymer which fuse together to form a structure. With each pass of the printing heads, the base on which the object is being made moves down a notch. In this way, little by little, the object takes shape. Voids in the structure and complex shapes are supported by printing a "scaffold" of water-soluble material. Once the object is complete, the scaffold is washed away.

Researchers have found that something similar can be done with biological materials. When small clusters of cells are placed next to each other they flow together, fuse and organise themselves. Various techniques are being explored to condition the cells to mature into functioning body parts—for example, "exercising" incipient muscles using small machines.

Though printing organs is new, growing them from scratch on scaffolds has already been done successfully. In 2006 Anthony Atala and his colleagues at the Wake Forest Institute for Regenerative Medicine in North Carolina made new bladders for seven patients. These are still working.

Dr. Atala's process starts by taking a tiny sample of tissue from the patient's own bladder (so that the organ that is grown from it will not be rejected by his immune system). From this he extracts precursor cells that can go on to form the muscle on the outside of the bladder and the specialised cells within it. When more of these cells have been cultured in the laboratory, they are painted onto a biodegradable bladder-shaped scaffold which is warmed to body temperature. The cells then mature and multiply. Six to eight weeks later, the bladder is ready to be put into the patient.

The Benefits of Bio-Printing

The advantage of using a bio-printer is that it eliminates the need for a scaffold, so Dr. Atala, too, is experimenting with inkjet technology. The Organovo machine uses stem cells extracted from adult bone marrow and fat as the precursors. These cells can be coaxed into differentiating into many other types of cells by the application of appropriate growth factors. The cells are formed into droplets 100–500 microns in diameter and containing 10,000–30,000 cells each. The droplets retain their shape well and pass easily through the inkjet printing process.

A second printing head is used to deposit scaffolding—a sugar-based hydrogel. This does not interfere with the cells or stick to them. Once the printing is complete, the structure is left for a day or two, to allow the droplets to fuse together. For tubular structures, such as blood vessels, the hydrogel is printed in the centre and around the outside of the ring of each cross-section before the cells are added. When the part has matured, the hydrogel is peeled away from the outside and pulled from the centre like a piece of string.

The bio-printers are also capable of using other types of cells and support materials. They could be employed, Mr. Murphy suggests, to place liver cells on a pre-built, liver-shaped scaffold or to form layers of lining and connective tissue that would grow into a tooth. The printer fits inside a standard laboratory biosafety cabinet, for sterile operation. Invetech has developed a laser-based calibration system to ensure that both print heads deposit their materials accurately, and a computer-graphics system allows cross-sections of body parts to be designed.

Some researchers think machines like this may one day be capable of printing tissues and organs directly into the body. Indeed, Dr. Atala is working on one that would scan the contours of the part of a body where a skin graft was needed and then print skin onto it. As for bigger body parts, Dr. Forgacs thinks they may take many different forms, at least initially. A man-made biological substitute for a kidney, for instance, need not look like a real one or contain all its features in order to clean waste products from the bloodstream. Those waiting for transplants are unlikely to worry too much about what replacement body parts look like, so long as they work and make them better.

| "[The] biggest challenges right now, for any solid organ, is . . . the blood vessel supply."

Some Artificial Organs Are Years Away from Viability

Anthony Atala, interviewed by Marissa Cevallos

In the following viewpoint, Anthony Atala asserts that artificial organs are years from being a viable alternative to donor organs. According to Atala, simpler structures such as skin, windpipes, and bladders have successfully been created in labs and transplanted into patients. However, he explains, solid organs such as kidneys are not yet viable because it is more difficult to replicate their blood vessel supply. Atala is the W.H. Boyce professor and director of the Wake Forest Institute for Regenerative Medicine and chair of the Department of Urology at the Wake Forest University School of Medicine in North Carolina. Marissa Cervallos is a writer for the Los Angeles Times.

As you read, consider the following questions:

1. What is the first way to create organ tissues, as explained by Atala?
2. According to Atala, what organs are in the second level of complexity?

3. How many tissue and organ types are being developed at the Institute for Regenerative Medicine, as stated by Atala?

The windpipe transplanted into a terminal cancer patient in Sweden is garnering much buzz—and small wonder. The surgery marks the first time a trachea grown from a patient's stem cells and seeded onto a synthetic, rather than a donor, structure has been transplanted in a human. And it saved a 36-year-old man's life.

The trachea isn't the first organ born in a lab—and experts say there are many more to come. We talked to Dr. Anthony Atala, a pioneer in the field who in 1999 transplanted the first of several synthetic bladders into young people with bladder disease.

Atala now directs the Institute for Regenerative Medicine at Wake Forest University; in March [2011], he and colleagues announced they'd transplanted laboratory-grown urethras in five boys.

Advances in Transplants

In this edited transcript of a phone interview, he elaborates on the significance of the latest transplant and explains why some other organs will be more difficult to craft in the lab.

[Marissa Cevallos]: What is new in the trachea transplant that hadn't been done before?

[Anthony Atala]: It's another advance. He [Professor Paolo Macchiarini of the Karolinska Institute] had done a segment of a trachea before. He has made it a larger segment.

The scaffold he used before, the biological material he used before, was a donor organ where they took the cells away and they put the patient's own cells. This time they did the same process, but they created a scaffold, a spongy scaffold.

Basically, there are a couple of ways of creating these tissues. One of the ways is to take a very small biopsy from a patient's own tissue, grow the cells outside the body, and then place those cells back on that mold that replicates the patient's organ.

Now the mold can be either something you create, something you weave like a piece of material, or it could be a donor tissue that you take the cells off and add cells to it.

What other organs have been made in the lab?

There are several organs. We did the bladder. We are 12 years out for using molds in bladders. We are seven years out in urethras, an experience just published. We showed that we transplanted urethras, using their own cells, but using molds.

Organs Have Different Complexities

Which organs are next, and which will take more time?

At this point, there are four levels of complexity.

The first level are the flat structures, like skin. They are the easiest to make because they are flat.

The next level of complexity are tubular structures, like the blood vessel, the windpipe. They are usually acting as a conduit, allowing blood or air to go through.

Next are hollow non-tubular organs like the bladder or stomach because they have to act on demand. They have much more complex functionality.

The most complex are the solid organs like the heart. They require many different cell types.

At this point, we've been able to do all the first three: Flat, tubular and hollow non-tubular. Skin, urethra, windpipes and bladders. Solid organs are most complex.

The fourth level—that's going to take time—that's still years away.

There are definitely more in the pipeline. At our institute we're working at over 30 different tissue and organ types. There's definitely a long list of organs that are scheduled to go into patients.

It's just a matter of getting more tissue types and more patients treated over time.

There Is a Major Need for Kidneys

Which organs will have the biggest clinical impact?

Well, of course for any patient who needs this tissue, it's a major clinical impact. If you need a specific tissue, it's a big thing.

The kidneys by far, if you look at the need—90% of the patients on a transplant list are waiting on a kidney. That's a fourth category. We are absolutely, working very hard on that.

What are the biggest challenges in making these organs?

Biggest challenges right now, for any solid organ, is basically the vascularity, the blood vessel supply. There are a lot more cells per centimeter in solid than flat tissue, and therefore, a lot of what needs to be done—how do you keep so many cells fed.

In the solid organ, if you can picture the branches of a tree, and then the branches have branches, and those branches have leaves, it's a very complex branching system. If you can picture the leaf being the tissue and the tree being the blood vessel supply tree, it's a complex organization so you have blood flowing through the tiny cell.

How did you react when you heard about the latest transplant?

We were very pleased to hear about this work because it just represents advances in the field and further validates the fact that these technologies may have a role in treating larger numbers of patients in the future.

> "Bioengineered stem cells . . . could be
> the game changer with regard to organ
> and tissue transplantation."

Stem Cells Could Solve the Organ Donation Problem

Andre Terzic, Brooks S. Edwards, Katherine C. McKee, and Timothy J. Nelson

In the following viewpoint, Andre Terzic, Brooks S. Edwards, Katherine C. McKee, and Timothy J. Nelson contend that stem cells could be used to create new organs. According to the authors, these cells come from a variety of sources, including embryos, umbilical cords, and bone marrow, and can also be bioengineered. They further argue that by using the patient's own stem cells, the risk of rejection is eliminated. Thus far, this technology has already been used to replace tracheas. Terzic is the director of the Center for Regenerative Medicine at the Mayo Clinic in Rochester, Minnesota; Edwards is the director of the Mayo Clinic Transplant Center; McKee is the operations manager of the transplant center; and Nelson is the E. Rolland Dickson scholar in transplant medicine at the clinic.

Andre Terzic, Brooks S. Edwards, Katherine C. McKee, and Timothy J. Nelson, "Regenerative Medicine," *Minnesota Medicine*, May 2011. Copyright © 2011 by Minnesota Medicine. All rights reserved. Reproduced by permission.

As you read, consider the following questions:

1. What are pluripotent cells, as defined by the authors?
2. According to Terzic et al., what are some of the adult stem cell therapies that have been developed?
3. What is the "ultimate goal of regenerative medicine," in the view of the authors?

Transplant medicine has laid the foundation for the emerging field of regenerative medicine, as the central aim of transplantation is replacing defective tissue with functional tissue in order to heal patients with end-stage disease. Over the years, tissue and solid-organ transplantation have been used to treat patients with otherwise incurable diseases such as leukemia, cirrhosis, end-stage kidney disease, and cardiopulmonary failure. Although transplantation has proved to be extraordinarily successful for some patients, the limited availability of appropriate organs and tissues and the problem of rejection have created a need for new strategies to meet the demands. Regenerative medicine offers potential solutions to these critical challenges.

Once, stem cell research and solid organ transplantation were separate endeavors. Materials science and developmental biology have bridged those fields, creating the new field of regenerative medicine. The initial application of regenerative medicine occurred five decades ago when hematologists began using bone marrow-derived stem cells as a replacement for defective progenitor cells. Advances in cell, tissue, and organ engineering have since led to new possibilities. Today, a variety of regenerative applications are being used and tested. In many cases, standards of care and best practices have yet to be established for cell-based regenerative therapies; however, clinical trials conducted by reputable institutions are actively enrolling patients in order to accelerate the translation of these promising applications. Regrettably, unproven therapies also are being marketed directly to patients, who may need to travel to other countries to get them.

As a result of the increased awareness on the part of patients, clinicians increasingly find themselves having to provide opinions about these therapies, some of which may be harmful or inappropriate for certain conditions. Thus, primary care providers and other specialists need to be informed about the state of regenerative medicine and emerging therapies that hold promise as well as those that are merely hype.

Exploring Stem Cell Research

Stem cells are the building blocks of regenerative medicine. As research on stem cells progresses, new information is becoming available daily regarding breakthrough technologies that will have an impact on our ability to translate stem cell science into clinical products and services. Regenerative medicine largely draws from four stem cell populations that function as tissue progenitors: embryonic stem cells, perinatal stem cells, adult stem cells, and bioengineered stem cells. Each cell type has unique properties.

As their name implies, embryonic stem cells are stem cells derived from embryos that are the product of in vitro fertilization. These cells are pluripotent, meaning they can differentiate into all adult tissue types. Because of their differentiation capacity, embryonic stem cells are suitable for deriving tissues that are difficult to obtain such as retinal pigment epithelial cells lost in macular degeneration and other tissues damaged by disease. However, the ethical and social considerations surrounding the use of embryonic stem cells continue to foster debate and challenge our legal system.

Perinatal stem cells are derived from umbilical cord blood. Although it is frequently discarded after birth, umbilical cord blood can be stored in private facilities or in public biobanks for later use in treating diseases such as leukemia. Perinatal stem cells are considered multipotent—that is, they can differentiate into many but not all tissue types.

Adult stem cells are present in many tissues including bone marrow, adipose tissue, and circulating blood. Unlike embryonic stem cells, adult stem cells are considered multipotent or oligopotent because their differentiation potential is restricted. This class of stem cells is most commonly used for treating lymphoma, leukemia, or autoimmune diseases that require cytotoxic treatments followed by rescue of the hematopoietic lineages and immune system. Currently, mesenchymal cells, which are derived from adult sources such as bone marrow or adipose tissue, are favored in clinical applications because they are widely accessible and because they have multipotent differentiation capacity, favorable growth characteristics, and an encouraging safety/efficacy record in clinical transplantation.

Bioengineered stem cells are a recent development. Scientists have been able to create induced pluripotent stem (iPS) cells using ordinary tissues such as the fibroblasts obtained from a dermal biopsy. With reprogramming or by applying genes typically expressed in embryonic tissues, adult fibroblasts can undergo a dramatic transformation and be reset to look and feel like embryonic stem cells. In other words, bioengineered iPS cells acquire the traits of pluripotent stem cells and the ability to differentiate into all types of tissue. These cells could be the game changer with regard to organ and tissue transplantation, as their use could offer a virtually unlimited renewable pool of tissues derived from the patient's own cells, eliminating the problems of donor shortages and rejection. They also offer a way around the ethical and political concerns associated with embryonic stem cell technology. Since the advent of iPS cell technology, bioengineered stem cells have become a source for progenitor derivation, tissue-specific differentiation, and repair in preclinical studies.

Clinical trials using adult stem cells to treat diverse conditions have established that this approach is safe and practical; early results of treatments for ischemic heart disease show promise. Therapies using umbilical cord blood stem cells, embryonic

Stem Cells Have Helped Heart Patients

Real progress has been seen in therapies derived from adult stem cell research. For one thing, [David] Prentice explained, "repairing the existing, damaged organ in the body replaces the need to do a whole-organ transplant." Several thousand heart patients have been treated with adult stem cells and subsequently taken off transplant waiting lists.

A study released last December [2009] in the *Journal of the American College of Cardiology* described how stem cells from bone marrow were used to help repair heart damage. And at the annual World Congress on Anti-Aging Medicine & Regenerative Biomedical Technologies last December, Zannos Grekos, MD, director of Cardiac and Vascular Disease for Regenocyte Therapeutic, showed the successful engraftment of stem cells into damaged organs and subsequent regeneration of tissue.

Daniel Allott, "A Vexing Problem,"
Catholic World Report, *July 15, 2010.*

stem cells, and tissue-specific progenitors derived from adult stem cell populations are being developed for early-phase clinical studies.

New Uses for Stem Cells

A number of developments are enabling investigators to envision new therapies and applications. The advent of bioengineered pluripotent stem cells is particularly significant. The ability to re-create pluripotent stem cells from ordinary somatic tissues such as blood or dermal fibroblasts makes it possible to create therapies that might one day eliminate the need for allogeneic

transplantation. Tissues that have been created using iPS technology include dopaminergic neurons (to replace those damaged by Parkinson disease), beta cells from the pancreas (diabetes), cardiomyocytes (ischemic heart disease), retinal pigment
epithelial cells (macular degeneration or Stargardt disease), red
blood cells (hemophilia and sickle cell disease), and hepatocytes
(chronic liver diseases). At Mayo Clinic, we have pioneered the
use of bioengineered iPS cells for treating cardiovascular diseases in preclinical studies. We are now applying this technology
to ischemic and nonischemic cardiomyopathy and congenital
heart diseases. Furthermore, the ability to program human iPS
cells into glucose-responsive insulin-secreting progeny has been
recently refined.

Advances in materials science are opening new avenues of
research in regenerative medicine. Matrices produced from natural or synthetic sources now provide platforms for growing tissue grafts and even engineering organs. In fact, preclinical studies have demonstrated that it is possible to decellularize organs
and leave behind only the extra-cellular matrix backbone. This
natural three-dimensional scaffold provides a framework for
progenitor cells to engraft and recreate the structure and function of organs such as the myocardium. The ultimate goal of this
work is to one day build replacement organs.

Such breakthroughs are setting the stage for new clinical applications. One of the most innovative ones was a whole-organ
replacement of the upper airway. Using a decellularized scaffold from a cadaver trachea, a team of clinicians, scientists, and
engineers repopulated the matrix with mesenchymal stem cells
derived from the patient's bone marrow. After months of re-
construction in the laboratory, the trachea was surgically transplanted in the patient without requiring immunosuppression.

In addition to such therapeutic applications, regenerative
medicine may also lead to better methods of testing pharmaceuticals. As part of safety testing, all new pharmaceuticals must
be evaluated for their toxicity. With the ability to produce hu-

man tissues using bioengineering processes, we may be able to test drugs in the laboratory before they are administered to the patient. For example, scientists are now testing cardiotoxicity of certain drugs using bioengineered cardiomyocytes.

Regenerative medicine also may help identify patients within the transplant population who will have more aggressive disease or who may be at risk for complications following organ transplantation. In other words, we may be able to use bioengineered constructs in the lab made from tissue from the patient's own body to predict such things as the long-term effect of exposure to immunosuppression medications. This ability to identify deficiencies in the tissue-renewal process also may be useful for creating individualized therapies for a variety of other diseases as well.

Regenerative Medicine Promises Better Treatment

Therapeutic uses are the ultimate goal of regenerative medicine. First-generation technologies are currently being studied with the aim of defining safety profiles of biologic agents while determining their efficacy in order to guide next-generation applications. This work will no doubt expand the number and type of patients who can be safely managed with tissue or organ transplantation. Autologous and allogeneic stem cells obtained from adipose tissue, bone marrow or peripheral blood, or bioengineered stem cells are already being used in applications designed to improve tissue healing in patients with ischemic heart disease, liver disease, neurological disorders, endocrinopathy, progressive lung conditions, and dermal wounds. Mayo Clinic physicians and scientists are developing procedures and infrastructure to support and accelerate clinical trials related to human stem cell therapies.

Regenerative medicine is redefining the future for patients with end-stage organ disease. It promises better, safer treatment at earlier stages and the possibility of cure rather than palliation of symptoms. Because its applications cross all medical disciplines, realizing the full potential of regenerative medicine will require collaboration among experts from multiple fields.

Clinical services may need to be restructured as new products and services become available, and as those products and services do more than treat specific organs or diseases. In addition, hospitals and clinics may need to dedicate resources to the field in order to efficiently navigate the regulatory processes for investigational new drug applications, FDA (Food and Drug Administration) reporting, and monitoring the safety of their clinical activities.

In addition, they may need personnel dedicated to dealing with the growing number of patients inquiring about new treatments and services. All physicians will need to know about advances in regenerative medicine and stay well-informed of developments in bench research and clinical trials as well as the limitations of therapies. How the medical community responds may be the key to whether regenerative medicine fully realizes its potential for returning patients to health.

Periodical and Internet Sources Bibliography

The following articles have been selected to supplement the diverse views presented in this chapter.

Alex Ballingall	"Heart in a Box," *Maclean's*, November 21, 2011.
Dan Bilefsky	"Black Market for Body Parts Spreads Among the Poor in Europe," *New York Times*, June 29, 2012.
D.A. Budiani-Saberi and F.L. Delmonico	"Organ Trafficking and Transplant Tourism: Commentary on the Global Realities," *American Journal of Transplantation*, vol. 8, 2008.
Jim Burdick	"Face Transplants: Part of a Brave New World," *Transplant News*, April–May 2011.
Mark Cohen	"My Illegal Heart," *Men's Health*, April 2010.
Henry Fountain	"A First: Organs Tailor-Made with Body's Own Cells," *New York Times*, September 15, 2012.
Josie Glausiusz	"The Big Idea: Organ Regeneration," *National Geographic*, March 2011.
Jeneen Interlandi	"Not Just Urban Legend," *Newsweek*, January 19, 2009.
Aamir M. Jafarey, Farhat Moazam, and Riffat Moazam Zaman	"Conversations with Kidney Vendors in Pakistan: An Ethnographic Study," *Hastings Center Report*, May–June 2009.
Medical Ethics Advisor	"Organ Trafficking—Truth or Urban Myth?," October 1, 2011.
Hari Pulakkat	"Cells Of Hope," *Business World*, June 27, 2011.

For Further Discussion

Chapter 1

1. The United States Government Accountability Office (GAO) asserts that more cooperation is needed among the government agencies that oversee organ donation. Of the problems detailed by the GAO, which do you think is the most pressing? Please provide a detailed answer.

2. The viewpoints by Steven Reiss and by Lainie Friedman Ross and Benjamin E. Hippen concern biases that they believe exist in the allocation of organs. After reading the viewpoints, whose argument did you find most compelling and why?

Chapter 2

1. Anthony Gregory and Priya Shetty debate the merits of organ markets. Whose argument do you find more convincing, and why? If there were a legal organ market in the United States, would you consider using it as a seller or buyer? Please explain your answer.

2. Do you agree with Daniel Sayani's argument that presumed consent is a violation of individual liberty? Why or why not?

Chapter 3

1. After reading all the viewpoints in this chapter, what do you consider to be the most serious ethical issue surrounding organ donation? Please explain your answer, drawing from the viewpoints and any other relevant readings.

2. The viewpoints by Jennifer Lahl and by Erin Nelson and Timothy Caulfield use a popular book-turned-movie as the impetus for their arguments on "savior siblings." Have you ever read a book or watched a movie that influenced how you feel about a controversial issue? Please explain your answer.

Chapter 4

1. After reading the pair of viewpoints on xenotransplantation, do you think it could be a viable alternative to using human organs? Regardless of your view, what do you believe would be the biggest impediment (medical, ethical, or social) to using animal organs in human patients? Please explain your answer, drawing from the viewpoints and any other related reading.

2. The final three viewpoints in this book present arguments on how advancements in science and technology may or may not change the future of organ donation. Of these viewpoints, which one do you think offers the most convincing arguments? Why did those arguments stand out for you?

Organizations to Contact

The editors have compiled the following list of organizations concerned with the issues debated in this book. The descriptions are derived from materials provided by the organizations. All have publications or information available for interested readers. The list was compiled on the date of publication of the present volume; names, addresses, phone and fax numbers, and e-mail and Internet addresses may change. Be aware that many organizations take several weeks or longer to respond to inquiries, so allow as much time as possible.

Alliance for Paired Donation
3661 Briarfield Blvd., Suite 105
Maumee, OH 43537
(419) 866-5505 • fax: (419) 383-3344
e-mail: admin@paireddonationg.org
website: www.paireddonation.org

The Alliance for Paired Donation helps people in need of kidneys through the use of kidney paired donations, where one incompatible donor/recipient pair is matched to another incompatible pair. In other words, the donor of the first pair gives to the recipient of the second, and vice versa. The alliance is also a pioneer in the use of non-simultaneous extended altruistic donor chains (NEAD chains). News and articles are available on the website.

American Organ Transplant Association (AOTA)
Administrative Service Center
PO Box 418
Stilwell, KS 66085
(713) 344-2402
e-mail: aotaonline@gmail.com
website: www.aotaonline.org

The American Organ Transplant Association provides transplant patients and their families with the resources they need to cope with this costly and difficult surgery. Among the services they provide are free transportation to and from transplant centers, fundraising information, a medical assistance program, and a list of patient support groups. The website also features links to transplant centers and other sites that provide information on developments in organ transplantation.

American Society of Transplantation (AST)

15000 Commerce Pkwy., Suite C
Mt. Laurel, NJ 08054
(856) 439-9986 • fax: (856) 439-9982
website: www.a-s-t.org

The American Society of Transplantation is an organization of more than three thousand transplant professionals dedicated to issues such as education, advocacy, and research. AST offers a forum in which these professionals can exchange knowledge and expertise. Position papers are available on the website.

Association of Organ Procurement Organizations (AOPO)

8500 Leesburg Pike, Suite 300
Vienna, VA 22182
(703) 556-4242 • fax: (703) 556-4852
e-mail: aopo@aopo.org
website: www.aopo.org

The Association of Organ Procurement Organizations is a nonprofit organization that represents fifty-eight federally designated organ procurement organizations (OPOs). Serving more than 300 million Americans, AOPO provides education and information to OPOs and collaborates with other health care organizations. The association also works with members of Congress and several government agencies on issues relating to organ and tissue donation. Numerous links relating to organ donation are available on its website.

Children's Organ Transplant Association (COTA)

2501 West COTA Drive
Bloomington, IN 47403
(800) 366-2682 • fax: (812) 336-8885
e-mail: cota@cota.org
website: www.cota.org

COTA is a nonprofit organization that provides fundraising assistance and family support to children and young adults who need or have had a transplant. Since its establishment in 1986, COTA has raised more than $65 million and helped nearly 1,900 people. Press releases, videos, and an annual report are available on its website.

Donate Life America

701 E. Byrd Street, Sixteenth Floor
Richmond, VA 23219
(804) 377-3580
e-mail: donatelifeamerica@donatelife.net
website: donatelife.net

Donate Life America is a not-for-profit alliance of national organizations and state teams that aims to increase organ, eye, and tissue donation. The alliance helps develop donor education programs and facilitate donor registries. Its website includes facts and statistics about organ donation, along with stories about organ recipients.

Kidney Foundation of Canada

300-5165 Sherbrooke Street
West Montreal, QC H4A 1T6
(514) 369-4806 • fax: (514) 369-2472
e-mail: info@kidney.ca
website: www.kidney.ca

The Kidney Foundation of Canada works with representatives from the Canadian government and health-care industry to improve the rates of organ donations. It also encourages Canadians to become organ donors and discuss their wishes with their families. Annual reports, fact sheets, and brochures can be found on the foundation's website, including the fact sheet "Eating Guidelines for Diabetes and Chronic Kidney Disease" and the brochure "Deceased Organ Donation: Let's Talk About It." Statistics on organ transplantation and waiting times are also available on the website.

Living Bank
PO Box 6725
Houston, TX 77265
(713) 528-2971
website: www.livingbank.org

The Living Bank was established in 1968 in Houston and is the United States' first organ donor registry. Its goal is to educate people about the need for organ donors and to advocate for donors and their families. The Living Bank currently has an organ donor database of 2 million people in all fifty states.

National Network of Organ Donors
PO Box 223613
West Palm Beach, FL 33422
(866) 577-9798
e-mail: info@tnnod.org
website: www.thenationalnetworkoforgandonors.org

The National Network of Organ Donors aims to eliminate the issue of liability from the decision to donate organs. It seeks to do this by lobbying the US Congress to pass laws that will give doctors and hospitals immunity from being sued by family members who are challenging a patient's intent to donate organs. The network also aims to collaborate with hospitals and other transplant listing organizations and establish a national database of organ donors. Statistics about organ donation are available on the website.

United Network for Organ Sharing (UNOS)

700 North Fourth Street
Richmond, Virginia 23219
(804) 782-4800 • fax: (804) 782-4817
website: www.unos.org

UNOS, a private, nonprofit organization, has a contract with the federal government to manage the nation's organ transplant system. Its responsibilities include matching donors to recipients on the national transplant waiting lists and maintaining the database for every transplant that occurs in the United States. In addition, UNOS oversees the Organ Procurement and Transplantation Network (OPTN). UNOS also publishes the bimonthly magazine *Update*, and the website has fact sheets and data about organ donation.

US Department of Health and Human Services, Division of Transplantation (DoT)

200 Independence Ave. SW
Washington, DC 20201
website: www.organdonor.com

The Division of Transplantation is part of the US Department of Health and Human Services. DoT oversees the organ and blood stem cell transplant systems in the United States as well as initiatives to increase organ donation. In addition, the division conducts a public awareness program with the goal of increasing donations. The division's website has links to organizations and electronic resources on organ donation.

Bibliography of Books

Firat Bilgel

The Law and Economics of Organ Procurement. Cambridge, UK: Intersentia, 2011.

Katrina Bramstedt and Rena Down

The Organ Donor Experience: Good Samaritans and the Meaning of Altruism. Lanham, MD: Rowman & Littlefield, 2011.

Scott Carney

The Red Market: On the Trail of the World's Organ Brokers, Bone Thieves, Blood Farmers, and Child Traffickers. New York: William Morrow, 2011.

Steve Farber and Harlan Abrahams

On the List: Fixing America's Failing Organ Transplant System. Emmaus, PA: Rodale, 2009.

Anne-Maree Farrell, David Price, and Muireann Quigley, eds.

Organ Shortage: Ethics, Law, and Pragmatism. New York: Cambridge University Press, 2011.

Sara Fovargue

Xenotransplantation and Risk: Regulating a Developing Biotechnology. Cambridge, UK: Cambridge University Press, 2011.

Reg Green

The Nicholas Effect: A Boy's Gift to the World. Bloomington, IN: AuthorHouse, 2009.

Petr T. Grinkovskiy, ed.
Organ Donation: Supply, Policies and Practices. Hauppauge, NY: Nova Science Publishers, 2009.

Sherine Hamdy
Our Bodies Belong to God: Organ Transplants, Islam, and the Struggle for Human Dignity in Egypt. Berkeley: University of California Press, 2012.

David Hamilton
A History of Organ Transplantation: Ancient Legends to Modern Practice. Pittsburgh: University of Pittsburgh Press, 2012.

Steven J. Jensen, ed.
The Ethics of Organ Transplantation. Washington, DC: Catholic University of America Press, 2011.

Andrew A. Klein, Clive J. Lewis, and Joren C. Madsen, eds.
Organ Transplantation: A Clinical Guide. Cambridge, UK: Cambridge University Press, 2011.

Hal Marcovitz
Organ and Body Donation. Edina, MN: ABDO, 2011.

Franklin G. Miller and Robert D. Truog
Death, Dying, and Organ Transplantation: Reconstructing Medical Ethics at the End of Life. New York: Oxford University Press, 2011.

Janet Richards
The Ethics of Transplants: Why Careless Thought Costs Lives. New York: Oxford University Press, 2012.

Sally Satel, ed.

When Altruism Isn't Enough: The Case for Compensating Kidney Donors. Washington, DC: AEI, 2009.

Maria Siemionow

Face to Face: My Quest to Perform the World's First Full Face Transplant. New York: Kaplan, 2009.

David Talbot and Anthony M. D'Alessandro, eds.

Organ Donation and Transplantation After Cardiac Death. Oxford, UK: Oxford University Press, 2009.

Dick Teresi

The Undead: Organ Harvesting, the Ice-Water Test, Beating Heart Cadavers—How Medicine Is Blurring the Line Between Life and Death. New York: Pantheon, 2012.

Paula T. Trzepacz and Andrea F. DiMartini, eds.

The Transplant Patient: Biological, Psychiatric and Ethical Issues in Organ Transplantation. Cambridge, UK: Cambridge University Press, 2011.

David L. Weimer

Medical Governance: Values, Expertise, and Interests in Organ Transplantation. Washington, DC: Georgetown University Press, 2010.

Beth Whitehouse

The Match: "Savior Siblings" and One Family's Battle to Heal Their Daughter. Boston: Beacon, 2010.

T.M. Wilkinson

Ethics and the Acquisition of Organs (Issues in Biomedical Ethics). New York: Oxford University Press, 2012.

Index

CPSIA information can be obtained
at www.ICGtesting.com
Printed in the USA
FFOW031551300513
1231FF

9 780737 763331